Property Negotiation

Mark Harrison BA, MA, MBCS

First published 2006
This edition 2007

Mark Harrison limited.
9, Malham Close,
Maidenbower,
West Sussex,
RH10 7JD

ISBN: 978-1-84753-845-1

This document was created using openoffice.org – a free office suite worth upgrading to.

Author photo courtesy of ric bacon.

WARNING

The value of property, like any investment, can go down as well as up. You should never invest without seeking professional advice. Neither the authors nor the publisher of this book accept any responsibility for actions taken as a result of reading this book. The worked examples used are for illustration only and the results achieved from a negotiation will depend on the circumstances and aspirations of the parties to that negotiation as well as the level of skill of the parties.

All of the case studies in boxes are factual, based on the authors' experience. However, the names of the participants have been omitted or changed, both to protect the privacy of individuals, and to respect the confidentiality of clients of Mark Harrison ltd.

About Mark Harrison

Mark Harrison was educated at Eltham College, London and Balliol College, Oxford. Graduating in 1992, he worked for some of Europe's leading companies in a series of increasingly senior IT roles, with responsibility for negotiating multi-million pound contracts.

He married Mary in 1995. In parallel with their careers, they built a property portfolio in London and the South East of England.

Their daughter was born in 2002, and their son in 2004. When their daughter was 6 months old, Mark quit his job, and started as a 5-day-a-week father. He now works an average of 2 days a week as a consultant.

About Mary Harrison

Mary Harrison was educated at the Weald School, Billingshurst and New College, Oxford. Graduating in 1993, she spent a short time working for an insurance company, before moving to the UK's leading firm of occupational psychologists, where she was responsible for system design.

She went on maternity leave in 2002 while expecting their daughter, and decided not to return to work. She continues to work as a systems designer for a few days a month, but prefers the challenge of bringing up her children.

About Mark Harrison limited

YourNegotationExpert.com is a trading name of Mark Harrison limited - a specialist company that helps clients maximise their profitability. This is done through a mix of training courses for their staff, and specialised direct assistance where clients prefer, on a consultancy basis.

For more information about using a consultant to assist you in your own negotiations, please email sales@yournegotiationexpert.com

Acknowledgments

- Dona for editing this, many times – thank you.
- Jonathan Histed, for getting Mark interested in property as a teenager, and for helping us both through many years.
- Rachel Byford for making Mary believe that she could try new things.
- Calum Morrell for help both in technology and ethics.
- Vanish Patel for the right advice at the right time, repeatedly.
- Parmdeep Vadesha for being a total guru.
- Kim Brown and Lisa Orme for believing that Mark had something to say that was worth listening to.
- Darryl Mattocks for kicking Mark out of his complacency, and subtly disguising the kicking with some excellent dinners.
- Hugh Jones for leading by example.
- Ric Bacon for the picture.
- And, in alphabetical order;
    - Gaynor Udeshi
    - Jenny Millington
    - John McCloy
    - Mark Hegan
    - Mark McCall
    - Paul Worthington
    - Peter Hutchinson
    - Richard McCabe
    - Roger Whittaker
    - Stuart Moore

Table of Contents

Introduction

We Don't Negotiate Any More

Imagine the scene. You are in the supermarket, doing your shopping, and you get to the till.

"That comes to £32.12, please," says the checkout guy, reading from the till. You look down in horror as you realise that you only have £30 in your pocket, and your credit card is maxed out.

Do you:

- A: Apologise and say that you only have £30, so put something back.
- B: Say, "Sorry, I forgot something," and head off, as if to the shelves, but then exit without being spotted.
- C: Say, "Will you take £30 for that?"

If you're like most people, the concept of offering less than the marked price for a basket of groceries probably fills you with horror. You know that the person on the till has no authority to offer you a discount, and will have to get a manager.

By the end of this book, you won't be asking for a discount for cash at the till, but you will, hopefully, understand that the supermarket owners have already used two negotiation tactics against you by the time they ask you for that £32.12.

In other parts of Europe, haggling over price is still the accepted social norm, but not in the UK. As a result of this, many people in the UK typically haggle over just three things:

- Their car
- Their house
- Their pay rise

Unfortunately, in these three situations, you are the amateur negotiator up against the professional. The car salesman, the Estate Agent, and the middle manager have all typically received negotiation training as part of their jobs, and know all the tricks to use against you.

As such, it's an area where it is worth spending some time learning and training. After all, would you expect an amateur, who had played tennis once or twice a year, to win a game against a tennis pro?

This book concentrates on the negotiation scenarios that you will encounter as a Property Investor. However, many of the principles and most of the tactics are far more widely applicable.

Except we do!

Having claimed that we don't negotiate, we now have to draw a new distinction. Of course, we do negotiate, we just do it without realizing that that is what we are doing.

Consider the following three lines:

- Dad, I need to borrow the car this weekend.
- We're facing pressure from our competitors, which means that we need to keep a tight rein on expenses this year.

- This house is worth £200,000.

All of these lines aren't actually statements of objective fact. They arc opinions, and can be regarded as opening positions in a negotiation.

"Dad, I need to borrow the car this weekend."

It's obvious that the person asking for the car (presumably a teenager) has a strong desire for something. Possibly it's that they would like to borrow the car for the whole weekend to go away with friends.

Possibly, however, it's that they would like to borrow the car for the Saturday night to take a new partner to the cinema, but know that if they ask you for the car for the weekend they can let you beat them down to just Saturday.

"We're facing pressure from our competitors, which means that we need to keep a tight rein on expenses this year."

This statement is almost entirely void of useful information.

Every business has competitors, and every business wants to keep control of its expenses – we don't actually need anyone to point this out to us.

In fact the statement translates, in many cases as, "We are laying down the groundwork to give our staff low / no raises, and stop our suppliers being able to increase the price of their goods and services."

"This house is worth £200,000."

The property market is a market.

That means that the value of something traded within that market (a house) is defined not by experts or central planners, but by what a buyer is prepared to pay, and whether the vendor will accept that price.

Typically, bald statements of 'Market Value' are made by someone who is trying to sell something – either a vendor or their agent trying to sell the property, or, more subtly, a buyer trying to 'sell' the deal to a mortgage company to get a loan.

Property purchases are widely touted as 'the biggest purchase you'll ever make'. Actually, for most people their pension fund is (hopefully) the biggest purchase they'll ever make. House purchases, whether for living or investing, are however the biggest headline transactions that most people make. As such, they are the one area in which it is possible to make or lose thousands of pounds extra profit in a few minutes work.

It's worth noting that the phrase 'I'm not negotiating here' is, itself, a negotiating position as the following example demonstrates:

Promotion Time

A few years ago, before he set up his own business, Mark was working for the web division of a large company, when Clive, his boss, unexpectedly resigned to go to another company.

Two days later, Mark was called in to see Colin, the CTO, who started out by offering Mark the job. Colin offered Mark a salary of £80,000 per year, a substantial raise from his previous salary of just over £60,000.

Mark, however, had suspected he might be the one chosen for the promotion, and had done a bit of research in comparable salaries, and countered that £85,000 might be a more appropriate figure.

Colin cut him off, saying, "I'm not negotiating here," and went on to explain that the salary had already been agreed with the HR department.

Ten minutes later, Mark walked out of the room with the original £80,000, but with an additional £4,000 per year in car allowance.

Mark grew up in London, commuted to work by train and tube, and had not taken a driving test at the time!

Learning To Learn

By the end of this book, however, you should know the tricks, or tactics, of negotiation.

You may, of course, decide that some of them are 'dirty tricks' that you would not feel comfortable using. This is absolutely fine – in these cases the purpose of this book is to teach you to recognize when those tricks are used against you, and what to do to counter them.

However, whether using tactics, or countering them, more skill is not going to come through reading this book alone – when it comes to improving your skill there is no substitute for actually trying to negotiate.

Before you start making offers on properties though, it is worth refreshing some key points.

Firstly, if (in England and Wales) you make an offer to buy a property, and then decide not to proceed, then you have effectively blown your reputation, and you will find it hard to be taken seriously again by Estate Agents, Mortgage Brokers and others who hear the story.

Secondly, if (in Scotland) you make an offer to buy a property, this has serious legal consequences and you can be sued if you subsequently don't proceed.

However, you have to start negotiation somewhere.

It is an odd fact of life that most people realise that physical training will stretch muscles, and as the muscle fibres grow, there will be some discomfort – whether you go to the gym, run, swim or ride, there's always a need to push yourself. However, in mental activities, many people are scared to try things that are even a little bit uncomfortable.

Mental activities have much in common with physical ones – to get better you have to go through the discomfort until the 'muscle' grows (until new neural connections are made in your brain.) You wouldn't try to lose some weight by EITHER still sitting in front of the TV all day OR by setting out after ten years of TV watching to run a marathon that afternoon. Instead, you'd start by doing a 5 minute run in the morning, and over a few months build up to a longer run by doing a little more each day.

In the same way, you need to train your mind to work more effectively by doing a little more each day, rather than storming into your boss's office on Monday morning, and demanding a 40% pay rise.

If you're really uncomfortable asserting yourself, start by looking for negotiation opportunities, even if you don't feel confident enough to actually try out the tactics at the time. You may not want to ask your boss if you can come in a couple of hours late because you need to go to the dentist, in return for which you'll work extra hours in the evening... but at least consider it rather than booking that half day holiday out of your annual leave entitlement.

Keep an 'I could have negotiated' diary for a few weeks, and each evening, look back over the day, and consider when you might have asked for a little more, and been able to offer a little more in return.

Then, pick an opportunity, and try a tactic out.

You used to, all the time

Anyone with small children will realise that the average three-year old has no trouble whatsoever with the idea that they can ask for things (although, fortunately for us parents, they don't have the negotiation skill or position to get what they want every time.)

Our three-year old demonstrates her ability to ask for a little bit more on a daily basis.

The call of "bed-time," is never met with, "OK," but always something like, "I'm busy," which she's learned is a good way to distract us by then asking what she's doing, which buys an extra five minutes...

... this is before the, "Which pyjamas shall I wear?", "Where have I left my teddy bear?" and, "I need a water pot!" tactics.

Before You Go Into A Negotiation

In this section, we'll be assuming that the negotiation is to purchase something – specifically a property. However, the principle stands when going into negotiations with tenants, Letting Agents, or tradesmen.

Before you start, you need to know two critical pieces of information:

- What is the most I'm prepared to pay at the end of the negotiation?
- What is the right number to open with?

Obviously, the first question needs to be flipped round before you go into negotiation with tenants: What is the least I'm prepared to accept at the end of this negotiation?

When we're buying property to let out, the figure we always use is that of Cash on Cash Return (CCR).

We work back from that to set a maximum purchase price.

To calculate CCR, we need to know several things:

- The purchase price
- The rent expected to be received
- The other fees, both in buying and letting
- The mortgage rate
- The intended Loan to Value (LTV)
- The tax rate you will pay on your rental profit

Cash on Cash Return is simple to outline, but long-winded to calculate. The simple explanation is that

$$\text{CCR} = \frac{\text{The cash you get back each year}}{\text{The cash you put in}}$$

Typically 'The cash you get back each year' is:

Rent (including allowance for voids)

- Letting Agents fees

- Maintenance expenses

- Interest

- Tax

And 'The cash you put in' is:

The deposit

+ Legal fees

+ Cash required for immediate improvements (if any)

+ Purchase taxes (SDLT)

As an example, consider these figures:

Asking Price:	£140,000
Rent:	£795 / Month
Void Allowance:	2 weeks per year
Legal Costs on Purchase:	£600
Letting Agent Fees:	10% + VAT
Maintenance Expenses:	5% of Rent
Marginal Tax Rate:	40%
Loan to Value:	85%
Cash Required for Improvements:	£500
Mortgage Rate:	5%
SDLT:	1%

From this we can calculate a 'cash required' if we paid the asking price:

Asking Price:	£140,000
Loan to Value:	85%
Deposit required:	15% (=100%-85%LTV)
Therefore Deposit:	£21,000 (15% of £140,000)
Cash required for improvements:	£500
Legal Costs:	£600
SDLT:	£1,400 (1% of £140,000)
Total Cash Required for Purchase:	£23,500

Next, we need to calculate the cash generated:

Rent:	£795 / month
Void Allowance:	2 weeks per year
Annual Rent after voids:	£9,173
Letting Agent Fees:	£1,078 (10% +VAT of £9,173)
Maintenance expenses:	£459 (5% of £9,173)
Borrowing:	£119,000 (85% of £140,000)
Interest:	£5,950 (5% of £119,000)
Profit Before Tax:	£1,687
Tax:	£675 (40% of £1,687)
Profit After Tax:	£1,012

This gives a CCR of only 4.3%:

$$\text{CCR} = \frac{\pounds 1{,}012}{\pounds 23{,}500}$$

Most sophisticated investors set a 'hurdle rate' which they need to achieve before considering any investment. Our hurdle rate is currently set at 20%, so it is clear that we would need to do rather better than the asking price on this property.

Sadly, calculating back from the hurdle rate to a 'maximum price' is a bit more complex, simply because some of the inputs, like SDLT, are not fixed numbers, but instead depend on the purchase price.

As such, the easiest way to work out the price you can afford to pay is to set up the calculations on a spreadsheet, and run a 'what if', plugging in different purchase prices and seeing what the CCR would be.

There is a spreadsheet to help you do this, available as a free download at our website – www.yournegotiationexpert.com/bonus

If you had set a hurdle rate of 20%, and can't do anything to affect the achievable rent, then the maximum purchase price comes out at about £76,000. This is clearly a massive reduction from the asking price, and it is most unlikely that negotiation alone would plug the difference.

However, to achieve this hurdle rate, we look for properties that can be substantially improved and then refinanced.

When we were working full time though, we weren't in a position to look at such things, and settled therefore for a hurdle rate of 'inflation plus 5%', which in days of 2% inflation means, of course, 7%.

To achieve a CCR of 7% means that we can afford to pay no more than £123,000. On a property with an asking price of only £140,000, this is the kind of discount that can often be achieved through careful targeting and good negotiation.

The utterly vital point to reinforce is that we may well NOT be able to negotiate down to £123,000 in this case. If we are unable to do so, then we HAVE to walk away from the deal, or admit that we are not going to reach our own financial targets on this investment.

You can't win 'em all

Skill at negotiation isn't enough to get every property for the price you want. Part of the skill is knowing when (and how) to walk away, but more about that later.

With an asking price of £140,000, and a maximum price we can afford to pay of £123,000, we need to set a starting price. Ideally, the starting price should be rather lower than the maximum price we can afford to pay – so that 'splitting the difference' would still leave us at a price we could afford.

However, in this case, this would give an offer price of £106,000, which may be so low it scares off the vendor all together, and stops them even considering a negotiation.

Sometimes this is the right approach. You may take the view that it is better to scare off 9 out of 10 vendors straight away and only invest serious time with those who are not fazed by such offers. However, you may find that doing this ends up with you making large numbers of offers, and never buying anything.

Other times, you have to trust your judgement and make an offer that sounds reasonable, perhaps in this case £119,000, and rely on your negotiation skills to make the vendor come down rather more than you will come up.

Spot when it happens to you

When we were selling a flat in Kent, we believed that a fair price would be £110,000. We therefore set the asking price at £119,000.

The first few offers that came in were for £90,000 and £95,000, from two different buyers, both of whom had told the Estate Agent they were investors.

Immediately we got the low offers, we knew that we were up against professionals rather than new investors.

We were able to react accordingly – by not taking any offence at the offer, but dropping the asking price by a few hundred pounds.

Neither of the potential buyers came back with a counter-offer, but we sold the flat a few months later – for £111,000.

Mark met Andy, one of the 'low-bidders', a little later, when he was emptying the flat just prior to completion, had a good conversation about the local market and took a quick tour of one of Andy's other flats in the block. Sure enough, Andy turned out to be an old hand, with a large portfolio in the area.

Negotiation Principles

Principle No 1 - What Are You Trying To Achieve?

What are you trying to achieve? For the majority of this book, I am going to use examples around buying houses, flats, or property. The reason for this is no matter what type of investor you are, you are going to need to buy some property at some point. If you are a buying and selling investor - buying property to refurbish and then selling it on, or buying property to sell on quickly; you will need to get involved with selling as well. Actually, the tactics for selling are the same. Just that you need to read the other part of the script.

As a 'Buy to Letter', it is more likely that you will, over the next 10 to 20 years, be buying properties but rarely actually selling any of it. Hence concentrating on examples of buying property will probably be more useful to you.

Level One

Simplest Level – what I call the Level One Goal. You are looking to buy a property. However, if you go into a negotiation just thinking, "All I need to do is make a purchase..." - then you are setting yourself up to fail as an investor. To make a profitable business as an investor, at the very least, you have got to be at, what I call, Level Two.

Level Two

Level Two Goal - you are looking to make a purchase, and at a price that will make you money.

Now, to distinguish between an Investment and a Speculation. For me an Investment is something that will give a positive cash flow and will definitely put money into my pocket. A Speculation is something that will **only** make me money, **if** the market does certain things; like goes up by 15% a year. Now on the one hand, it is very unlikely that the market will go up 15% next year. On the other hand there are many people out there selling the kind of property "rescue" deals that only make sense if we are in a market that **is** going up 15% each year. Some of these are the Off Plan Investments, which only stack up, if the market is rising by 15% to 20% a year over the next year or two.

So making a purchase at Level Two, you look to:

- make a purchase
- **and** at a price to make you a profit

Level Three

This book relates to the property market in England and Wales, as that is the law I am most familiar with.

I am not talking about in Scotland, where you write up an offer, or America where you write up an offer and sign up a contract on the very same day, or Australia or South Africa where yet more rules apply.

We're talking about England or Wales.

What do we know about England and Wales? That from agreeing a price, the vendor has a long period in which to change his or her mind. It may be shorter, but typically it is six to eight weeks. This is the period from agreeing terms up to the Exchange of Contracts. Once the contracts have been exchanged, the vendor can't pull out - at least, not without having to put up a lot of their own cash as a penalty.

But until then, the vendor can change his or her mind. Now we have all heard this magic word "Guzumping" so we all know it happens.

So my view is that you want at least a Level Three, where you look to:

- make a purchase
- at a price to make you a profit
- **and** when you walk out of the negotiation with the vendor happy, leaving the vendor thinking that **they** have got a good deal, and leaving the vendor **not** motivated to start another set of negotiations, with another prospective buyer, because they feel that they have really been pushed to the wall.

Consider now

That you've agreed to buy two identical houses, next door to each other, numbers 1 and 2 Acacia Avenue, for the same price, from Adam and Bob respectively.

With Adam, you've acted the aggressive negotiator, somewhere between Arnie and Gordon Gecko. Not only have you got a great price out of Adam, but he knows it. He knows you're a tough cookie, and that you have really beaten him down. You spent a lot of time haggling, to really get him to concede all over the place.

Bob, on the other hand, knows that he was able to get a great deal out of you. You've worked really hard on the deal, and spent rather more than you wanted to, because Bob has done such a good job getting the best price out of you.

Now, remember, you've ended up with the same price on both purchases, and both have been put to the respective solicitors on the Thursday morning.

Late on Friday, Carol walks into the Estate Agent and says, that she really, really, really, wants to live in Acacia Avenue. She had seen the ads in the paper a couple of weeks ago. Dave the Senior Negotiator (look at that job title for a moment) says that he's just had offers accepted on both of the two houses. Both owners have asked him to take them off the market. However, Dave gets Carol's details to keep on file.

On Saturday, both Adam and Bob are shopping in the High Street, and decide to pop in to say, "Thanks," to Dave for negotiating their sales. Dave lets slip that there was another buyer who was asking for property in that road. How do you think Adam and Bob are going to react?

Well, a lot will depend on their personalities, and whether once they've 'shaken on the deal' they will stand by it.

However, Adam believes that he did badly, and may well be tempted to let her have a look. It's possible that, once Carol sees the place, she'll make an offer that beats yours, and you've either lost the deal, or have to up your price.

Bob, on the other hand, believes that he's been victorious, and has got a great price. There will be significantly less temptation for him to allow Carol to darken his door, because he doesn't think he'd do any better, and might run the risk of you pulling out and losing the great deal he already has.

So under the law in England and Wales, remember to keep the vendor feeling that they have done a good job otherwise there is a long period of time in which the vendor can back out and change his or her mind.

Level Four

Now I go a step beyond Level Three, to what I call Level Four – this only applies if you are buying through Estate Agents. Now I know it has become very fashionable over the last few years to talk about buying direct from vendors, finding motivated sellers, putting newspaper adverts in or joining clubs, which are basically syndicates - doing all these things to bypass Estate Agents.

I have found that many of my successful property purchases have come through Estate Agents, because they get to see a greater number of potential properties which are placed on the market. If you choose to buy through Estate Agents then I think you need to be looking to buy at level four:

- make a purchase
- at a price to make you a profit
- leave the vendor feeling that they have got a good deal out of you
- **and** leave the Estate Agent wanting to do business with you again

This is not an overnight thing. People often ask me how to build a relationship with Estate Agents. There is a chapter later in the book, which handles this in more detail, because building such a relationship with Estate Agents can prove extremely useful when you are an investor. Estate Agents will sometimes come to you first with the good deals, deals which they know meet your investment criteria. So I would make sure the Estate Agent doesn't feel: "That was hard work", that they have been hard done by, or that they have lost out in any way. This is actually an important part of what you are trying to achieve when you are buying property regularly through an Estate Agent.

Clearly, if you are aiming to buy direct from the vendor and bypass the Estate Agents altogether then you don't need to worry about this level. But whenever there is an Estate Agent involved make sure that they are happy as well.

Principle No 2 – Invest Time Not Emotions

This has been well researched in the academic world. It is generally accepted, that the longer someone spends in a negotiation, the more motivated they are to leave with an agreement rather than walk away with no agreement, having to start negotiations again with someone else.

Have you ever sold the house you lived in?

If so, I want you to cast your mind back to when you were selling that property. The Estate Agent phones up and says, "The couple who viewed last night. They have made an offer!" Your emotion level grew, and it is like a roller coaster ride for the next few days as you went back and forth before coming up with a price you could agree to. Most people really don't like this. Most people find it terribly uncomfortable, not what they like to do. If it is not part of their job, they are not used to negotiating big contracts. Even if they are, it is now their money, rather than the money of the company they work for, and it is very uncomfortable.

Once your emotions start coming into play, once your emotions start controlling you – you will make a worse deal. Moreover, you, as an investor, want to make sure that the emotional buildup is happening to the vendor and not to you, the purchaser.

The best advice I ever got, was from a Canadian property developer: "You don't make money with your head; you make money with your gut." Learn to control your emotions, don't let them control you. More cynically, if emotions are going to be working, as undoubtedly they will - make sure that they are working **for** your side.

Getting the vendor to invest more time in the negotiation is a classic way of getting them to invest more emotional capital – if that is the right word. The more emotionally tied up they are, the more the negotiations have gone back and forth, the more nights they spent thinking, "Is this going to go through?", "Are we going to get a price agreed?" - the more likely they are to accept that low price you offered. They are unlikely to then say, "Oh blow it!" as the idea of starting negotiations over again, to go through it all again the next week - is too much. Quite often, the difference in this can be literally thousands.

Principle No 3 – Remember Your BATNA.

BATNA is one of the four technical terms I use in this book. A BATNA, is a term from Academic Negotiation Theory, and stands for "Best Alternative To Negotiated Agreement".

The term comes from much research carried out by American Universities. It is primarily around employer/employee union relations, and it works on the logic that when the workforce is on the verge of going out on strike, or even worse, has gone out on strike - you need to come to an agreement. The alternative to not reaching an agreement is that everyone loses.

- The company loses because they no longer make the goods or provide the services that the customer pays for.
- The employees generally end up losing because it means ultimately someone's having to pay, even if that is the union for the period that they are out on strike.
- The union loses typically because their coffers are being drained if they are providing supporting funds for their members that are out on strike.

In Property Negotiation it is just as important, but it is much simpler as you don't need to go through this analysis of what will happen if you don't. What you have got to remember is that every time you negotiate to buy an Investment Property, you always have an alternative. That alternative is to go and look at the next property, go and view the next house, go and get the next set of details, go phone up on the next property, and make a low offer on that.

If I look at the figures on the properties I have purchased over the last ten years. I reckon that for every property I have ended up buying – I have had a HUNDRED sets of Estate Agent's details, and probably gone to view TWENTY of them. Typically I have made offers on only TEN, and ended up buying just the ONE.

Those last two figures are key, for every negotiation I have gone into - 90% have not resulted with me buying the property. Going through TEN negotiations and buying ONE blindingly good purchase, that is going to be putting a few hundred pounds into my pocket every month from now until my great, great, grandchildren's retirement, is better than making ten offers, buying five of them and finding out that four of them are mediocre, or worse, some are costing me money each month. There is never an excuse for buying a property as an investment that is going to cost you money.

You may choose to buy things that are like that, but bear in mind that the word is not 'investment'. The word is 'toy' or the word is 'speculation'. If it puts money in your pocket, it is an Investment. If it costs you money because you want it, it is a Toy. Or if it might make you money only if the market does something, or might cost you money if the market does something else, it is a Speculation. The extreme form of speculation is called a 'gamble'; effectively they are the same word. An Investment is something that will make you money. In property negotiation you are looking for investments not speculations.

There is only one time, in property negotiations, that you are looking for toys and that is when you are looking for the house that you actually want to live in for the next ten, fifteen, to twenty years. Then it is fine to buy what you actually want rather than a property that will make you money. There are more important things in life than wanting more equity in your own home. But for investment properties use the word investment.

Principle No 4 – Know How Much You Can Afford To Pay.

Working this out is very, very simple. You just need to remember the two important Real Estate Gurus of the twentieth century: The Spice Girls and Lionel Ritchie.

The Spice Girls are important, as they taught us all we need to know about choosing an investment property, with their song 'Wannabe' - remember that tag line that went, "So tell me what you want, what you really really want."

What the Spice Girls were doing was basically giving a lesson to all Property Investors – in fact to all business investors and owners generally. Which is start by working out what the market wants.

Now I have a very simple three-point plan for running a business. It is:

1. Work out what your prospective customer wants.
2. Work out whether you can deliver it to them profitably.
3. Make a decision; if you can deliver it to the customer profitably DO IT, if you can't deliver it to them profitably DON'T DO IT.

This plan seems to work well but I know many people who use a completely different set of plans. In fact my first few businesses were:

1. Work out what I know how to make.
2. Make it.
3. Then work out whether I can sell it.

My first business was a classical recording business, making CDs of early music. Our first CD was "The Lute Music of John & Robert Johnson". For those of you not familiar - John & Robert Johnson were contemporaries of William Shakespeare, a lot of their music was, apparently, written to accompany some of the original performances of William Shakespeare's plays. Our recording was played by Lynda Sayce who is Britain's premier lutanist.

I suspect that, apart from me, no one reading this has purchased a copy of this CD. As it turns out, there isn't a large market for early lute music. Worldwide with seven different exporters, to date, we sold fewer than two hundred copies.

It is a great CD, she is a great lutenist, the music was fantastic for the genre, but there was not a big enough market to sustain it as a business.

I learnt a few things in that business and basically the key one is to work out what the market wants - then work out whether you can deliver it profitably – then work out whether you should do it.

So if the Spice Girls taught us anything it is that you need to remember that you have customers.

We don't like the word customer in the landlording or in the 'Buy to Letting' business. We like to call them tenants. Tenant is a technical term, it means customer of a landlord. You make your money in landlording when somebody pays money to live in your property for a month or six months, or whatever period you are letting it out for. You make money when a customer pays you money.

If you are purchasing a property to sell on, you too have customers. They are called the buyer, the person who will buy your property from you, when you are finished with it. So shouldn't you do what you would in any other business, start with market research? Work out - what tenants want. Work out - what buyers want. I'll stick to landlording, as it is what I know far better.

You need to begin with market research. Where do you do the research? Do you find out want tenants want, via your Estate Agent? - NO – Estate Agents are there to sell you property, and will tell you whatever they think you need to hear to enable that property sale to go ahead.

Letting Agents are where you find properties that people want to rent to live in. I start by asking the Letting Agents in my area, "What type of property can I bring you, that would just bring a smile to your face?".

Which types of property, would they not need to waste their marketing budget on. The properties where they wouldn't need to send a colleague round with a digital camera in order to photograph for the advert. Which properties would they be able to just reach into their bottom drawer, and have five prospective tenants' phone numbers to call, and have them come round to view it, that evening?

What I have found is, that in nearly every area I have invested in, there are some roads, some properties, some types of properties that people will always want to live in.

Work out what it is that people want to buy/rent from you - what your customers want to buy from you, what your customers want to rent from you. Then work out if you can deliver that to them at a profit. Don't start like most people do, when starting to invest in property - by looking at what is for sale!

That is the landlord equivalent of working out that I can make early music CDs. That is NOT the landlord equivalent of market research, and learning how to use it effectively.

One little word about Letting Agents, ask your Letting Agent the following questions:

1. "Hi I am a potential landlord and I am thinking of buying a two bedroom flat in that block. How much rent will I be able to get?"

Make a note of that number. Then the next day phone them up again but ask:

2. "Hi I am thinking of moving into the area. I was driving around at the weekend, and I saw these roads – can you tell me how much it is likely to cost me to rent a two bedroom flat in these kinds of areas?"

See whether they give you the same answer. What you find is that the good Letting Agents will give the same answer; whether they think that you are buying or renting. The bad Letting Agents are sometimes a much as £200 more generous in their estimates of potential rent values to landlords as they are in how much they can expect to pay to prospective tenants.

There is just one other question to ask the Letting Agent, apart of how much the rent will be, from those two different perspectives. That is:

3. What section of the letting market do you specialise in?

There are in Crawley, where I am based, a number of different Letting Agents – I don't deal with Martin & Co, not because I have heard anything bad about them, but because all they let are fully furnished properties on a fully managed basis. I, for my own various reasons, like to manage my own properties and I prefer to let my properties unfurnished, therefore Martin & Co are a complete mismatch for me. There is no point in asking Martin & Co what people would pay in rent, for a certain type of property, as it would be entirely misleading. Their target clients aren't going to be interested in what I have on offer.

The other place to do market research is newspapers. Get the local paper and go to the property pages. The first half, the property sales – ignore. Go to the second half, the letting pages. Look at the various Letting Agents, look at what is available, because that will give you an idea about prices. But also look at what is not there. You, hopefully, will know the area, so you know the make up of properties. You know if there are a lot of two bedroom flats, lots of mid terraces etc. If one type aren't advertised, then what it could often mean is that they don't need to be advertised. It may mean that when a two bedroom flat in that block comes up the Letting Agent only has to phone around half a dozen people, who he knows are looking to live there, and they never need to waste this advertising space for that type of property.

Below Market Value

So you've had the Spice Girls – "So tell me what you want, what you really really want." The other Property Investor Guru is Lionel Ritchie, with that marvellous song "Is it BMV you're looking for?" Now I guess these days most potential investors are familiar with the term BMV – Below Market Value. Where investors purchase a property for less than it is worth.

The trouble is; what on earth do I mean by Market Value? There are some people, like Parmdeep Vadesha, who have written some very sensible stuff on how you go about achieving that. However there are many people who throw around the term Below Market Value, and don't have a clue what it means, or worse deliberately misrepresenting what they are offering, to be Below Market Value.

The thing is – you remember that BATNA was one of the four technical terms you need to know - here come the other three in quick succession.

In order to establish a Market Price for something you need a market. What markets give are:

- Liquidity
- Fungibility
- Transparency

These are explained as:

Liquidity

Liquid is basically what the Stock Market gives. If you have something to sell, it provides the market. What the market guarantees you, is a buyer – it can't guarantee the price, it can guarantee a buyer.

Likewise, if you are a buyer, a liquid market gives you a seller.

> If I have 1,000 BP shares and I want to sell them, I go to my broker and say, "I want to sell my BP shares this morning." The broker will say, "Certainly sir." The broker then phones back in ten minutes or half an hour, "Yes they been sold the funds will be available in three days."

Is the property market Liquid – if I have the details on a flat I want to sell this afternoon, can I phone up my property broker and get a sale today?

Well, there are a few circumstances where you could get a same day sale.

The first is an auction – it is possible to sell a property that day. However, the vast majority of auction buyers will only bid on properties they have seen and been able to research in advance. Most auction houses would be terribly unhappy to find a seller turned up on the morning of the sale with a set of property details in hand asking them to squeeze it into the sale.

The second is the fabled 'cash buyer' - the person who really can turn up at a property, agree a sale, and pay that afternoon. If truth be told, most of the 'quick buyers' (myself included) who will agree to buy a property that day will want to leave themselves at least a couple of weeks to get the legal details sorted out properly and make sure that the legal searches don't turn up anything seriously wrong with the property.

Overall though, the property market is NOT liquid.

Fungibility

Fungible – this means that if there are two items for sale that they are absolutely identical.

In the example above; any two BP shares are fungible, the only difference between them is the share number. They carry the same voting rights and dividend entitlement. If I have 1,000 BP shares and I want to sell only half of them. It does not matter which half I sell.

If you have two five pound notes in your pocket, it doesn't matter which one you pay with, obviously one has a different tag number on the bottom, but otherwise they are completely identical.

Is this true in Property? Again, no – 1 Acacia Avenue, and 2 Acacia Avenue may have different outlooks, they may have slightly different décor. One may have wooden floors, the other may have carpeting. They are not the same.

If you have two identical properties in a block of flats they can quite genuinely, be worth £50 or £100 different in monthly rental, depending on what floor they are on, or which side of the building they look out of. There is NO fungibility in the property market.

Transparency

Transparency – the third thing; when I sell my BP shares, my broker can see what other people are offering for BP shares. My broker has a computer screen with a hundred different bids on it and the computer automatically selects the best offer from the large number of people who are looking to buy BP shares at that moment.

It is transparent because, I can see all the prices that people are offering to pay, and so can everyone else interested in those shares, both buyers and sellers. Everyone can see all the up-to-date information on everything that is available, everything that is sought after and at what prices.

Is this true in Property – once again, no. At any given time, the Estate Agent has a snapshot of a few properties that they have sold that week, but doesn't know what other agents have sold for. The data is delayed, so while it's available later, it is not up-to-date at the time the deal is agreed.

So what is Market Value?

Market Value is not the Estate Agent's asking price. Many people who say, "I want to buy Below Market Value," think that they have got it when they suddenly get a 20% discount on the asking price. Then six months later, when the Land Registry figures come out, they realise so did everyone else.

Many people, particularly in the last few years, think that Market Value is the builder's list price, and that because they got a 20% discount and a gifted deposit that they have got themselves a really fantastic deal. Indeed there were plenty of people who thought that they were getting a really good deal when they got a 15% discount from the builder and when the Land Registry figures come out discover that they paid more than anyone else in that block did, for flats which were at the same price point.

The Market Price is what the stupidest person was prepared to pay. The most gullible idiot who will pay over the odds is the person who sets the Market Price. Because anyone with a brain on them will sell to the person who offers more, rather than to the person who offers less.

Market Price is not average price either. It is not the price at which there are a lot of buyers. Market Price is the price at which there is only one buyer who is willing pay just that much. That one person, who is able to pay or is willing to pay more, than anyone else potentially interested in that property.

So is it Below Market Value that you are looking for? - well yes and no. Yes, in that given two choices where you could pay more or less for something – you should always be looking to pay the least possible. But the trap that most people have fallen into in the last couple of years, is that they **think** that if a property is Below Market Value or they **believe** it is Below Market Value, it is therefore, an investment and a must buy.

I know many people who thought that they have bought at 'Below Market Value' only to find that they can't let it, they can't sell it, they can't offload it. Their great investment has cost them six months in holding costs and mortgage interest, and when they do sell it, it is only for a couple of grand more than they bought it for. They end up losing money on the deal.

Below Market Value is not enough.

Below Break-Even Value is the term that I use. This is the price you can buy something at, so that the income it generates will cover all your costs and leave you with a profit. That is the figure I certainly focus on – and not getting caught up in the 'Below Market Value' is the answer and the only answer.

The next question is: how do you workout the Below Break-Even Value? You need to do a couple of sums. These are not complex; if you can do division then you can work them out. An investment should generate a profit. A profit is simply the income it generates minus the costs it takes to run. If you are buying with a mortgage, the costs include all interest payments.

So what is the income? Well obviously income is the rent in the case of rental property. But remember - you don't see all that rent. Typically the Letting Agent will deduct their commission. Also, there is no rent when the property is empty. The income on a property, isn't simply the 'Oh, I'm told this property will let for £750 a month' multiplied by twelve – which makes £9,000 a year.

It is this amount take away 10% +VAT for the Letting Agent's commission, take away another 5% because the property might be empty two or three weeks in the year. Do these calculations very conservatively to work out your forecast of what the property will bring in.

Then look at your costs. For most of us, the biggest cost is the mortgage interest payment. You know how much you are borrowing and you know what your mortgage rate is, so you can work out how much the monthly interest will be.

You need to make an allowance for maintenance. I have found that assuming I am going to be paying 10% of my rent in maintenance costs, isn't far wrong. Generally I get away with figures less than that, but because of the area I am in, and the type of tenants I am targeting, I need to keep my properties in top notch condition. That means not letting things get shabby; replacing things more often than a landlord who is targeting DSS tenants would perhaps see the need to.

Allow for insurance. You want your properties insured, and your lenders will insist that you do. If you are letting unfurnished, this need only be buildings insurance. If you own one flat in a block, you might be offered a pro-rata portion of a larger policy, covering the whole block, by the Leaseholder.

Allow for other things, - the list is long: Gas Inspections, Electrical Certificates (it all adds to the costs), Service Charges, Leaseholder's Fees, Ground Rent Charges, other stupid charges, like: the fee the post office has to get post re-directed. The list goes on and on. Each year there is a new expense I haven't come across before, and I am not sure which category it comes under. Make allowance for those costs. Again, be cautious.

Then work out how much money the property will put in your pocket each month. The rent minus the letting fees etc., less the costs and maintenance etc.- is your profit.

You are looking for a good return on your money. If you put twenty thousand pounds in a bank or building society then, depending on where we are in the economic cycle, you can expect to earn interest on that money, of between 2% and 10%. Now if you put twenty thousand pounds down as a deposit on a property, don't you think that the return should be better than if you had just placed the money in a 2% interest investment account at the Halifax?

When I am looking at how much capital I am investing in a property, I look to make investments that typically give a return of 20% to 25% on my capital each year. I know there are more sophisticated things you can do. I have learnt a lot of things in terms of buying properties that needed doing up, spending a short amount of time refurbishing them, then refinancing them, and thereby reducing the working capital requirements.

There are also lease options which include agreements on how much rent the tenants pay each month.

At the end of the day, which ever way you do it, you need to keep track of how much of your money - your capital, is tied up by a property, and how much of a return that property is generating. As this creates for you your working capital for the next project.

So focus on the return on investment, not on the Below Market Value. Focus on the return on investment on properties where there actually is customer demand, not on the cheap price of properties where there is cheap property supply.

Remember, and keep to, your price

When you have worked out what you can pay - WRITE it down. Then straying into the realm of psychology, before its chapter, don't just say to yourself, "I am going to pay 175K for the property."

- Actually WRITE IT DOWN.
- SAY it **as** you write it down.
- RING it in a **different** colour.
- **Write** it rather than type it.

Now the reason for this is that it engages all your modalities. That is the different ways your brain processes information. By saying the £175K out loud, you are processing it through your auditory system. By writing down the figure, you are seeing it and processing it through your visual cortex. Also the actual act of writing out the numbers: One Seven Five Zero Zero Zero, engages the kinaesthetic part of your brain.

What you are trying to make utterly, utterly, utterly sure is that at every step of the negotiation process, you remember that amount. That it is inscribed in your memory, your heart even, to help ensure you don't go over it.

So that is Part One; making sure that your mind is utterly trained, and knows what the limit you can pays is – in such a way that it is so firmly anchored, you won't forget it, or be tempted to exceed it.

Principle No.5 - More Than Just Price

There is actually more to it than just the price. Hopefully, you have heard of the three things you offer as an investor. You are not just offering money. You are offering a combination of money, speed and security.

Most vendors start out by concentrating only on the price. And in a buoyant market, where buyers are keen to snap up property, they often have a selection of offers.

However, most of the time, the market is not buoyant. Vendors go for weeks without an offer, and start to question what they are trying to achieve. There are some vendors who need a sale quickly more than they need the best price.

The third thing you can offer is security. The vendor who needs a sale quickly is looking for reassurance that the deal is going to go through, and they are not going to have wasted a month for the so-called 'quick buyer' to pull out at the last minute. You need to provide assurances that the deal is not going to falter.

In some cases, there are other possibilities – vendors may want earlier moving dates, later moving dates, the opportunity to rent their own property back once they've sold it, and so on.

I once agreed a deal that gave the vendor use of the garage for a week after they sold. The house to which they were moving had chain problems and couldn't complete for another week – they were happy to move in with friends for the week, but needed somewhere to put their furniture.

Principle No.6 - Never Offer The Asking Price

The final Negotiation Principle may be a ploy or tactic, but I think that it is sufficiently important to make it a principle.

Never

offer

the

asking

price

Negotiation Principles

I feel strongly about this one – could you tell?

Never, never, never offer the asking price. It is the single biggest mistake that first time buyers make. Particularly if they think that the market is going up, they think, "I must offer the asking price."

I will explain later why it is an utterly stupid and destructive mistake.

Principle No.7 - Make Them Feel They've Won

In principle one, I talked about the importance of this. However, I think that it's worth re-iterating; because sometimes people who have followed principle one at the beginning of the negotiation let their guard down at the end and ruin things.

It can be very tempting, when you've just had some kind of success, to be very obviously pleased and happy. Whether this is helpful or not, is another question.

If you are jumping in the air because David Beckham has just scored another goal against Argentina, then this is probably going to be fine (unless you happen to be in Buenos Aires at the time.)

If you are jumping up and down making 'ca-ching' noises (as, worryingly, I've seen some new Property Investors do) then you are increasing the risk that you will get a last-minute 'I've changed my mind' phone call.

When you have just agreed a deal, it is far better to congratulate the other party than it is to celebrate. Good salesmen know this – and are taught to say things like, “It's a great car you've just bought,” or similar things, specifically to reinforce in the mind of the buyer that they've 'won'.

Even when the deal is over, and legally secure (because contracts have been exchanged, or your tenant has signed the AST and paid the higher rent), it is still better, long-term, to give credit to the other party. A tenant who chooses to renew in six months time will save fees, voids, and effort. A vendor who has just sold to you, and knows that you are an investor, may recommend you to a friend down the line, or you may ask them to supply a testimonial for future clients. These recommendations are rare through an Estate Agent, but it does happen, as does the converse – the vendor who tells people that they were beaten down in a deal.

Negotiation Styles And Personalities

Empowering Beliefs

Many things in life are objectively true or false, irrespective of what we believe about them.

For example, if you pick up a coffee mug, stand up, and let go of the mug, you will quickly receive a demonstration of the law of gravity, irrespective of whether you learnt enough physics to think in terms of 'attraction between two objects being proportional to their masses, and inversely proportional to the square of the distance between them'; or whether you believe, wholeheartedly, that gravity is a bourgeois plot to oppress the masses.

Alternatively, no amount of pressure group lobbying would convince even the most agile of politicians to confirm that, effective from the next session of Parliament, the sky would be red with purple spots.

Statements like, 'cups fall to the ground because of gravity' are objectively true (at least, to the level of our current understanding) and statements like, 'the sky is red with purple spots' are objectively false.

However, many things that we accept as 'true' or 'false' are either matters of opinion, or literally non-testable.

Consider the statement, “Shane Warne is the greatest cricketer alive today.” You might believe that it is true, you might believe that it is complete rubbish, or you might have no interest in the question at all. However, even the most ardent Andrew Flintoff fan would admit, in a quiet moment, that it was only a matter of opinion.

In between the two extremes lie a whole range of 'facts' that we act upon daily, as if they were true, without ever having explicitly tested them, or considered that they were only a matter of opinion.

Statements like, 'I'm intelligent', 'I'm hard-working' or 'I'm good looking' (or 'I'm modest') are more than just opinions – they are beliefs. A belief is an opinion that you act on, as if it were real.

The question about beliefs in these cases becomes not, “Is this a true statement?” but, “Will believing this make me more effective?” Beliefs that help you achieve your goals are called empowering beliefs.

Conversely, beliefs that stop you achieving your goals are called disempowering beliefs. The classic example of this is, the teenager who believes, “She'll want to dance with me,” and the teenager who believes, “She'll never want to dance with me.” The first teenager will ask the girl to dance, and the second will hang around with his mates all evening (even though the girl in question actually wanted to dance all along.)

Understanding that there are some things you believe, because they make you more effective, is a key to the psychology of negotiation.

Some of the things that we're presenting as principles are not things that you could ever test scientifically – however, they are things that we've discovered, time and time again, that make us more effective as negotiators.

> In the example in the Introduction, I knew that Colin was an experienced negotiator who would never have come into the meeting room with his final offer upfront. I believed that he was canny enough to have left himself some negotiating room.
>
> *That* made me believe that he was expecting me to make some counter-proposal. Believing that he was *expecting* that counter-proposal then made me believe that he would think *less* of me if I just accepted his first offer.
>
> Believing he would think less of me if I *didn't* make a counter-offer gave me the confidence to ask for an extra £5,000.
>
> What did you believe last time your boss offered you a raise?

A Short Parable. About Beliefs

There is a classic parable about this on the facing page.

Now it is a very obvious and easy parable but it does underline that there are some things which, if you go through life believing them, will not help you – as in the case of the parable where everyone in life is nasty and doesn't want to be involved with you, (you can call this a disempowering belief or a self-fulfilling prophecy, the term doesn't matter.) However, if you believe the opposite – in this case, that people are there to help you and will get on with you – then you will probably find that they do.

A man, who is hiking through the Himalayas, encounters a monk on the road between two villages. He asks the monk, "What are the people like up at the next village?"

The monk replies, "Where have you come from?" The hiker indicates the last village, and the monk then asks, "How did you find the people there?"

The hiker says, "They were really nasty – they didn't make me feel welcome, they just weren't interested in talking, and they didn't want me to get involved at all."

The monk says, "Well, my son, I fear that you will find the people in the next village are the same."

Then half an hour later a second backpacker comes up the same road, he asks the monk the same question, "What are the people in the next village like?"

Again, the monk asks, "How did you find the people in the last village?"

The backpacker replies, "I found them really friendly and welcoming. When I spoke to them, I respected their customs and traditions, and they were really fantastic, lovely people to be with. In fact I have stayed there three or four days longer than I had expected to."

The monk turned around and said, "You will find that the people in the next village are exactly the same."

They Need You More Than You Need Them

Now there is one very empowering belief in property negotiation; you need to go into the negotiation believing that the vendor needs you much more than you need the vendor.

Now, when you go into the negotiation you can't tell if it is true or false. Yes, you can do your research and find out whether they have certain characteristics that might make it true, but at the end of the day, you can never get 100% information before you start negotiating.

The thing is, if you go into every negotiation acting as if they need you more than you need them; that they will be willing to take Below Market Value offers, or deal really fast and so forth, when that happens to be true, you will get a blindingly good result. When that belief happens not to be true, although you acted as if they needed you more and they didn't, then you won't make a good deal. But then you wouldn't have done so anyway.

Acting in the negotiation as if they need you far more than you need them only works when it happens to be true. But we are not talking about union/employer wage negotiation where they have to get to an agreement. We are talking about do I buy this property? I buy the property only if:

- it is a great price, that meets my financial objectives
- it leaves the vendor happy
- it leaves the Estate Agent wanting to do business with me again

... otherwise I am quite happy to walk away.

If you have that empowering belief, you get much better results when the vendor does need you and actually find that you get no worse results when the vendor doesn't.

Conscious Versus Unconscious

The second thing I want to explore in psychology is conscious verses – and here the language changes depending on who you are talking to. Some people call it Subconscious; some call it Unconscious; some use the word Automatic.

When I run my training courses, I ask the people in the front row, "Who can catch?" I will then throw my mobile phone to them. Sure enough they catch it.

Then I ask if there is anyone who has at least first year university mathematics, and can solve simultaneous differential equations. Occasionally a delegate can. I do have a degree in mathematics, but would I still be able to solve simultaneous differential equations? Probably not. Don't be alarmed, as I explained earlier, so long as you can do division, that is the only calculation that you need to do, to make money as a Property Investor.

If you talk to a mathematician, or a physicist, about how you predict where the phone is going to be in time to move your hands to the right place to catch the phone; just predicting the motion of the phone is a simultaneous differential equation in four variables, let alone the equation needed to move your hands. Now I am guessing that the person catching the phone didn't first work out the equation, then solve it, to predict where the phone would be in time for them to catch it.

The delegate caught it because he has learnt to catch. The equations are being solved anyway, but rather than being solved in a conscious manner - by writing out the calculations with lots and lots of variables - there is a part of his brain, that over the last thirty years has got so good at catching objects that his hands will move **automatically**. Now I have a three year old daughter and would not throw my mobile phone to her, expecting her to be able to catch it. I wouldn't throw anything to her that could either hurt her or be damaged if she let it drop; because she is only three she hasn't yet learnt to catch reliably. We practice catching soft toys and things, and I throw gently, but she has not yet learnt to catch reliably. I am expecting however, that she will learn to catch things reliably sooner than she is able to solve simultaneous differential equations.

When you do something time and time again, when you get into the habit of doing it, you train part of your brain, get the synaptic connections working so that it happens automatically. That is how you start getting good at things.

There are a few skills in negotiating that we will cover in the next chapters, which you have to practice so that you do them automatically. If you leave it up to your concious mind, those one or two seconds that it takes your concious mind to do it, could mean that you lose the effect, and may run into problems.

By the way, there is a word for an automatic response that is empowering. That word is SKILL. That is what a skill is – something that you are able to do automatically and that helps you as you go through life. Whether that skill is singing, or catching at cricket, or negotiating, or investing, or marketing - or whatever it happens to be that you are good at - you probably got good at doing it, by doing it so many times that you manage to do it now without having to think it through every step.

So automatic actions (whether you want to call them unconscious or subconscious, but automatic as opposed to conscious) are a terribly important concept in anything you try to achieve.

Ethics

The next concept in psychology is about Ethics. Now I am a South London boy, and you may think Ethics is the county I think is just north of the Thames in London.

Obviously, though, I am talking about Ethics as in morality. What I am not going to do is to preach to you. I am not going to tell you what is right and what is wrong. I work on the theory that, if you are old enough to sign a mortgage contract or sign a deposit cheque, then you are old enough to have worked out, in life, what you are prepared to do and what you are not prepared to do.

And there are things in the ploys section, some of the negotiation tactics employed, which you, will think are dirty tricks. That you would not be prepared to do. The reason I am teaching you about them is so that you can recognise when they are being used against you. You need to recognise them for what they are; not to treat them as a true thing, that has happened, or something that has happened by accident, or anything other than as a negotiation ploy. They are something that the other party in the negotiation has decided to try on you.

There are some things which are clear cut, and people feel happy doing. However, there are some things which are very obviously dirty tricks, that no one I want to do business with, ever does. There are some things which are in a grey area in the middle. Whether you would be prepared to employ these tactics or not; that is the ethical question you need to answer for yourself.

Think About The Impact Of What You Say

The next thing about psychology is, "How will the other party react to my words or actions?"

I had a many great teachers at school: one was Mr Tatt[1], my Physics teacher. As well as teaching me about gravity in a way that I can remember twenty years later, but he had this fantastic phrase, "Flash of the blindingly obvious!" There are some things that you hear once and you suddenly think, "Yes of course." One of those about negotiating that really made sense to me is **think how your opponent will react to your actions.**

1 Mr Tatt died in July 2005, shortly before the first publication of this book. Sometimes, you never find time to say "thank you" to those who deserve it – in his case, however, I did. Requiset in Pace.

Think through, not just the effect that this will have on you, by making an offer or saying something, but also, what the response will be from the other party. Give thought to this before you say anything in a negotiation, before you take the next step, or make the next offer. This, by the way, is why you should never (or 99% of the time) offer the asking price.

Moreover, this is the straightforward beginner, just getting on the property ladder, mistake. I have a couple of friends in their mid-twenties, a year to year and a half ago, they were looking to buy a house together and get on the property ladder. They went out and looked at a bunch of flats. Found a flat that they liked, and they went to the Estate Agent the next day and said, "Yeah ,we really like it and we want to offer the asking price!".

What they had probably imagined, (though to be fair I don't know if they had even thought about it), is that the Estate Agent would phone up the vendor and say, "You know that couple who came round last night, well they have been in and they have offered the asking price." They thought the vendor would say, "Excellent, we have got our sale."

What do you think happens 99 times out of a 100 when a vendor gets offered the asking price straight away?

They think, "I should have asked for more!" The vendor may think that as they have achieved the asking price just like that, if they had asked for another ten or twenty grand, they could have come up another ten grand with a couple of days haggling. "If only I had started, by asking for twenty thousand more." Remember what I was saying earlier. What are you trying to achieve? You are trying to achieve a sale where the vendor is happy - as the vendor has six to eight weeks, before exchange of contracts, in which to change their mind.

Some vendors are honourable enough that, once they have reached an agreement, they will go through with it and there won't be an issue. But there are enough vendors out there, who will say to the Estate Agent, "Yeah! Okay we will take it off the market." However, should the vendor happen to bump into their Estate Agent, the following week, and the Estate Agent lets slip that there was someone else who was prepared to make a higher offer, the vendor might turn around and say, "Well what was it?" They might change their minds – with the best will in the world, it happens.

It also happens in negotiation with tenants.

I have had one prospective tenant who saw the place on a Friday evening at seven o'clock, who said "Yes, we would like to take this place. We will be in at nine o'clock in the morning at the Letting Agent's office, to sign the agreement."

The following day, I got a call from the Letting Agent – it turns out that the couple had had another viewing booked for later in the evening with another Lettings Agency. Although the tenants had tried to get hold of the other Letting Agent, to cancel the viewing, they had been unable to get hold of them to do so. They thought that it was only polite to turn up, to view the other property anyway, so that they weren't thought to be timewasters.

However, they stepped through the front door, and fell in love with the place. I had a very guilty phone call from the Letting Agent to say that, she was terribly sorry, but they had changed their minds.

Nevertheless, it can easily happen. Maybe they don't feel good about it, but vendors do change their minds. You have got to make sure that the vendor is not in a position to change his or her mind. The best way to do that is to make the vendor feel that he or she has won; instead of going in straight away and quickly offering the asking price, which is, more times than not, a great way to make the vendor feel that they haven't been asking enough. If only they had asked for a bit more, then they would have felt that they had done better. It is setting up the circumstances in which they might go back on their word.

A lot of people have come up to me in the past and said, "Well look! The mistake I made was, I should have offered the asking price on this one. Because I made on offer, and the next day someone else offered the full asking price; then got it. Now that property is worth much, much more than it was then."

The trouble with that is, with my scientist's hat on, we will never know! If they had offered the asking price maybe, the following day that other purchaser would still have said, "Yes, I know that you have been offered the asking price, but I will offer ten grand more. What do you say?"

What I believe, from having done it lots and lots of times, is that by offering below the asking price and allowing myself to be talked up, perhaps even up to the asking price, you do not set up the psychology in the vendor's mind, that they have been asking too little. Obviously you would only be talked up to the asking price if it met your investment criteria but anyway, you shouldn't make it your first offer.

Personality Type Assessment

Before reading this next chapter it is well worth taking time out to do the assessment. You will find in the appendices a quick psychometric assessment. (You can download additional copies at www.yournegotiationexpert.com/bonus)

You need to circle one word on each line, which best describes you. There are no right or wrong answers. It is your initial reaction which is often the most accurate, rather than any premeditated response. If you can't decide between two on one line, circle them both as it is the proportion in each column and not the totals which give the results.

Take about five minutes to go through the list. The first twenty will be easy and you will feel really good about them – this is because they are your strengths. However, the last twenty will be harder, as they are your perceived weaknesses.

TIMEOUT for the assessment. (Any problems with the words in the assessment please refer to the word definitions in the appendices).

Please do take time to do the test before reading on!

When you have completed the test, add up the number of circled words in each column: strengths plus weaknesses. Make a note of each total beside each column. This will show you what proportion of each personality type you are.

I had better explain what those columns mean, now hadn't I? Going across from left to right they are: Choleric, Sanguine, Phlegmatic, Melancholy.

Whilst those terms are not the most memorable, I know that there are some systems which use a similar test and assign different animals types to each, if I use the terms choleric, sanguine, phlegmatic, and melancholy (which are recognised psychometric terms) then you will be able to look them up on the Internet to find out more. These are the terms which the more serious sites and also text books will use. Therefore, you can find out more about them.

Choleric

I would not be surprised to see that the kind of people who have bought this kind of book are more choleric than the average population. By definition readers of this book are a self selecting type, just as Property Investors are.

So, you Cholerics, you are going to like this. You are action taking. You are extroverted. You are optimistic. These are all things that you like. Hopefully, those of you who are choleric, you are smiling in agreement. Not only are these good words, these are words that you feel really pleased to have used to describe you. If I say, he is a real extrovert, she is optimistic, you'll be thinking, "Yeah! That's good. That's great."

What you probably don't realise is that there are other people who, if I described them as optimistic, they think, "Oh! no!". Cholerics you should be really careful. These words tend to put a smile on your face when you hear them about yourself, however, there are other people who regard them as an insult and would hate to be described as such.

So Cholerics, you are action taking and optimistic. However, there are a couple of dangers which you need to be aware of in negotiations. You have a tendency to be so forceful, particularly if you scored very highly in the test, that you upset the other party and they will walk away. That is the extreme case.

The more insidious one is, because you are always thrusting ahead, always doing something, you are not willing to invest time. You have a tendency not to be willing to invest the time it takes to drag out a negotiation. You may want to get to a conclusion straight away. You want to make a decision this afternoon! Take it or leave it. Sometimes a negotiation is a game, that can take several days or even several weeks to play. Therefore, for you Cholerics that is something that you have got to be careful of.

If you are Choleric, what you have got to understand is, that you need to relax, take a step back. You have got to appreciate that sometimes relaxation is so important. That relaxation is such an important thing, that to accomplish it, you may need to plan for it. A Time-Out is what needs to be accomplished and deliberately planned for. A break of 24 hours IS the right thing to do - remember to allow the other party time to let their emotions get involved.

Phrased in those terms, the Choleric will understand the concept. You are delaying for 24 hours because that is the necessary next best step. Otherwise the choleric will say, "I need to have it done now." Understand that actually giving the other party time, in short, giving the other party time to sweat – is the aim. This is something that you would have no trouble doing as a Choleric. Giving the other party time to sweat is something the Choleric can understand, they can get their heads round this.

Wanting the decision now is the problem the Choleric needs to overcome. Plan it – I am giving them time to sweat. This tends to be the way the Choleric can accomplish it, and carry it through.

Sanguine

If you are Sanguine, you are even more extroverted. A really strong Sanguine is even more extroverted and outgoing than the strongest Choleric.

If you are Sanguine, you are optimistic. You are engaging. You are fun to be with. People enjoy spending time in your company. These are things that the Sanguine feels really good about, when used to describe them. The Sanguine thinks, "Yeah" and, "Aren't they really great things to be." But again, there are other personality types who think, "I would never want to be the centre of attention," who would never want to have the spotlight cast on them. So realise, just because you think that it is a good thing when describing you, that there are many other people who do not value the same characteristics that you value. Who aren't judging themselves against the same standards as you do.

The danger with the Sanguine is that they babble, they end up talking. Because of this, they may end up giving away too much by accident. You all know that information is power; I will talk about power in the next chapter. Sometimes as a Sanguine you might give away too much about yourself. Now I can't see you, but I doubt that I would see a face of denial if I could.

A more serious problem, especially if you are very strongly sanguine, is that you are real scatterbrain. You all know the terribly bubbly, doesn't know what day of the week it is, personality type.

They tend to be incredibly strongly sanguine. This can be great to have as a front person for your business but you actually need to have someone to take care of the details.

If you are very strongly sanguine you need to have a good secretary; a good personal organiser. I am strongly sanguine which is why I employ a secretary. My secretary gets me, with the correct equipment, to the correct place, and on time which, left to my own devices, I wouldn't. It is bad enough if you are going to a training course and are late – but if you as the speaker can't turn up on time, you tend not to get many referrals, or testimonials, or bookings.

As a Sanguine, there are two negotiation mistakes that you might make. One, (I kid you not), is forgetting what you agreed and offered the last time. Really, quite literally forgetting what it is that you had offered previously. At this point you need to get organised. WRITE everything down, get a notepad or organiser. Whenever you have a phone call scribble in the notepad a phone memorandum because you may not remember. The strongly sanguine should make a note of what they say.

The other problem the Sanguine has, is that they interrupt. They enjoy hearing the sound of themselves talking so much that they interrupt and cut others off, rather than listening to what is being said. Listening is just as important a part of communication as talking is.

It is terribly important for the Sanguine to WAIT and take a deep breath; actually realising that taking a deep breath and listening is really sometimes to your advantage.

If I find someone who is really strongly sanguine, I give them a really hard challenge like; go to a party, and don't say anything for the evening. What you find is that one person will ask, when they haven't said anything for the last five minutes, "Are you Okay?". More people will say, "Gosh they were really on form last night. It was really nice talking to them."

If you are Sanguine you actually talk far, far too much! You do not realise that listening will often accomplish far more than talking would.

Phlegmatic

Personality type three is the Phlegmatic. I'd be surprised if there were many people reading this who are predominantly phlegmatic because the Phlegmatic can't be bothered to buy these types of training courses. Either their partners have got it for them, or someone else has pushed them into doing it, or they are reading this type of 'stuff' as a favour to someone; not because they want to.

If you are phlegmatic, you are calm, you won't get flustered, you won't be hurried, you will avoid conflict. The Phlegmatic comes across as having really good and useful characteristics. The danger with the Phlegmatic is that they can be really indecisive, they don't get around to it. When I have done these tests before, you find that it is the Phlegmatic who says, "As if this test means anything." They are really unenthusiastic about it, they refuse to be pigeon-holed. They want to feel they can't be categorised.

If you are strongly phlegmatic you have got some great characteristics, but you have got some things to be careful of too. Now I keep this section about the Phlegmatic short; because they really don't like reading about themselves, they want to go away and think about it. The Choleric and Sanguine want to hear me talk on for hours about THEM. But the Phlegmatic wants a short little bit, which they can then go away and consider and take their time to think about later.

As a Phlegmatic, your biggest negotiation mistake is never getting started in the first place; you just need to discipline yourself to get started. This is a shame because, of all the personality types, the Phlegmatic is actually very good at the mechanics of a negotiation. They don't let their emotions get in the way, they are just prepared to let things go along at their own pace. The Phlegmatic will invest the time. The Phlegmatic has some of the strongest strengths for negotiating, when they get started. If they can be pushed into doing it - they are terribly, terribly good at negotiating.

In my construction business I had a partner who was very strongly phlegmatic and really hated negotiating. He's a trained engineer, a very good engineer, but he didn't like talking prices. He didn't like pushing people to make decisions. When customers came back asking to talk about prices, I would tell everyone that they had to talk to him. He listened to them, talked to them, and made it clear what he could and couldn't give up on price. He was very good at getting the deal closed and getting them to actually pay the original asking price and not 'cutting a deal' and giving away 10% or 15%.

In comparison, another salesman I know has no phlegmatic tendencies whatsoever. He gets through lots of business, but with very low margins. He consistently gives away every last penny of his negotiation room. He wants to turn round twenty deals and if that means cutting straight to his lowest point – so be it.

The Phlegmatic is actually a really great negotiator, if they can be bothered to get started.

Melancholy

The final type, the Melancholy; what is good about you? You are analytical, thoughtful, and detail conscious. Well, hey! Aren't they things we all need, to be able to run a business? We need people who are analytical, we need people who actually think about what we do and we need people who get all those little details completed, which end up with the deal actually working rather than never coming off.

The danger with the Melancholy, is that the Melancholy can see the downsides far easier than they can see the upsides. The danger of being too melancholy is that you are over analytical and you get analysis-paralysis. You are so good at doing the analysis and see so many potential problems that you don't ever go ahead. It tends to take melancholy people a long time to get started in something. Once they are into something and have built up some momentum, and they can see it working, then they tend to be very good at doing it again and again. But the actual getting started in the first place is the problem.

So the biggest negotiation mistake that the Melancholy is likely to make is that they will spend so much time going through looking for reasons on why it might go wrong that they will always err on the side of caution, and walk away. They may find that two years later they still haven't bought any properties. So rather than ending up settling for one in ten properties, you decide that none of the twenty were really good enough. What I suggest to you Melancholies, is that you actually look at both sides of the analysis. You not only look at what would happen if you did it, but also look strongly and analyse what would happen if you didn't do it.

It is very easy if you are melancholy to get hung up in the, "No I am not going to buy this property, because this might happen: I might have voids, something might go wrong, it might be overvalued, I might not be getting Below Market Value, or all these things." You have to think about what would happen if you carried on for the next five years doing the same thing – you would still be in the same place. How does that compare to buying your first investment property?

Getting the Melancholies to analyse both sides of the equation can be terribly, terribly difficult. Actually getting them to focus on the downside of NOT getting started at all, of never coming to an agreement, tends to be the way you can get Melancholies to start building a business of any sort.

To Summarise

So just to summarise each personality type and recap – this is how you explain what you are:

- If you are Choleric you say, "I am Choleric" and if you are strongly choleric you say, "I am Choleric, damn it!"
- If you are Phlegmatic you say, "You can call me phlegmatic - as if."
- If you are Melancholy you say, "Well actually I'm only 82% Melancholy. I'm also 14% Phlegmatic and I have a 4% Sanguine tendency."
- If you are Sanguine you say, "Oh what was it... It began with an S...... training course in London, so and so was there. No, can't remember, but it was an S anyway."

Hopefully these sketches will remind you what the four personality types are and will help you to relate better to each. Personalities types are important for two reasons;

1. The most important thing, especially if you are strongly one or other type, is that it can be very difficult to realise that the other party doesn't see life the same way you see life. The other party isn't trying to achieve the same things you are. They have a completely different set of criteria they are trying to optimise: 'things they are trying to get done' as the Choleric would put it, 'stuff that turns them on' as the Sanguine would put it. So understand what the other party values, understand that it may well be different to what you would value.

Sometimes it is very obvious what personality type the other person is, sometimes it isn't. It is worth remembering that they aren't necessarily seeing life through your set of glasses.

2. The other thing is to understand your own tendencies and weaknesses and specifically to look out for the negotiation weaknesses; they are things that you actually want to focus more conscious effort on avoiding. Your strengths, they are the automatic responses. It is the weaknesses where you need to make your conscious mind work harder to reduce the tendency, so that a better response becomes more automatic.

Negotiation Power

If you read negotiation textbooks, there are many sources of power that are talked about. You find that there are three sources of power which are not very common in property negotiation: Reward, Coercion and Reverent Power... which I will quickly explain first.

The sources that are important in property negotiation are: Position Power, Charm Power, Information Power and Situation Power. So I will explain these in greater detail.

Reward Power

In the more general world of negotiation there are things like Reward Power; for when you are negotiating with your boss on something like a pay rise or taking an extra day off next Tuesday. Your boss has the power to award that raise, or give the day, or not. Typically, you will find that that doesn't apply to property negotiation.

Coercion Power

If you are negotiating with a Police Officer who has pulled you over for something, he actually has fairly strong Coercion Power. If you don't play the game to his or her rules then you could run into a lot of trouble.

Reverent Power

The Pope has a lot of reverent power. Many people are interested in doing what the Pope says because they look up to him, because of who he is and they respect him. You seldom end up buying a property from the Pope.

Position Power

Position Power is when someone tries to take the upper hand in a negotiation because of who they are. They try to position themselves as having the reins, of being the ultimate decision maker, or having the best information, not because they actually have the best information or are the decision maker, but because they have the position which might make you believe it.

In property negotiation, this type of power tends to be taken by the Estate Agent. The Estate Agent is often saying, "I know how much this property will sell for! Because I'm an Estate Agent." Any of you who have ever tried to buy or sell through an Estate Agent, will know that this is true. "I know this will sell for..." "I know this is worth...." They are trying to use their position to influence you, as the buyer, into offering more because you will respect their experience as an Estate Agent enough to believe them.

Not a good trick to fall for. It may work with their client, the vendor, but it should never work with you as a Property Investor and buyer. You should never be respecting the Estate Agent as an expert in the property market. There should only be one expert in your property negotiation and that person is you. You should have done enough research so that you know more about what is going on than anyone else in the phone call, or in the negotiation room.

Charm Power

Charm power is when people will help you because they like you, because you are affable, because you come over as nice. Quite often you find you get a better price because they like you. The Sanguine tends to do this naturally.

In reverse, something that many American styled negotiators think is a good idea, is to go in criticising everything. Saying, "That's no good!", "That is broken!", "There is a problem there!". What they are doing straight away is putting off the vendor, making the vendor poorly disposed to them.

I prefer to make viewings with the Estate Agent so I can't influence the vendor in this way. Or, if I do go round with the vendor, I always try to be complimentary, and say things like, "That must really suit you.", "You must have put a lot of work into it."

Not things which would make them think, "Oh so it is going to be worth more!", but things which give them a favourable impression of me. "That is really interesting what you have done with that bedroom." Not something that can change the value I place on the property. I do not subscribe to the theory in negotiation, that you go in being critical and giving yourself ammunition to drive the price down.

In my experience that hasn't worked as well as being nice, being pleasant, and making them think, "Oh, this is a tough negotiation, but at the end of the day he's a nice guy, I'd quite like to make a deal with him."

"He's a really nice guy" is something you want your opponent to be saying about you. If 'opponent' is the right word in a negotiation, which I think it is.

Information Power

The third is Information Power. This is where, as I was saying, the Estate Agent must not be the expert.

If you are looking to buy a property, you need to know what comparable properties have made. You need to know what similar properties have sold for, are selling for, are being advertised for. You need to know how long the property has been on the market for. You need to know what the vendor's circumstances are. You need to know all these kinds of information. You need to know on what basis your offer is being made.

When people ask "How did you arrive at that figure?" I say, for example, "I need to look at what the rental income will cover in terms of borrowing, and that is how I have arrived at this figure." You need to be able to back it up. You should make sure that you know your answer and have an explanation, so it doesn't just look like you are haggling.

Now when it comes to information power, you need to know some numbers - and trust not the Estate Agent for he is not your friend. The Estate Agent is the paid agent of the vendor. (I will be explaining more about Estate Agents in a later chapter).

The one area where you should never trust the Estate Agent is how much rental income you can expect the property to achieve. It is so important, that I will say that again, Estate Agents do not tell the truth.

They are optimistic, they are generous in the figures, they will say, "Well I'm not really a rental expert but I think that it will let for £900 a month." – you can take from this that the real figure might be closer to £600. Don't trust them, make sure that you do your research so that you go into every negotiation knowing as much information as possible.

That is what gives you the power; the best information.

Situation Power

The final point is Situation Power. Situation power is best summed up by the phrase "They need you more than you need them". In some situations it happens that, due to the circumstances, the situational power is on only one side.

The classic example of this is getting locked out of your hotel room in your underwear, and the receptionist asks, "I will need to see some form of identification before I can issue a duplicate key." That is

Situation Power. It is not about what is right, it is about who is in control.

Talking to traffic wardens, they hold the Situation Power, because at that moment they may or may not give you a parking ticket, depending on how you deal with them. Realise when the traffic warden is about to issue you a ticket - they have Situation Power.

In property negotiation it is down to how much the vendor really needs you, compared to how much you need them. Understand that you have the Situation Power when you are in a position to give them what they might need very, very quickly. That is when those really low offers are accepted. When you can pick up true bargains.

Negotiation Ploys

In the feedback I have received from the One Day Courses I run, it is clear that people are surprised that the whole day is not just devoted to the tactics used in negotiation, or the language you use, or the things you say.

However, by the end of the day, or certainly a week later, after the information has been absorbed – the response is: "I am glad it wasn't."

Understanding *why* you are saying certain things will help to make it happen. If I just started off by saying "Look say this…" or "Trust me on this..." most people would have trouble doing it, without the reasons behind the action. The chapters on the principles and the psychology have been building up to this chapter.

For each ploy or strategy I am going to explain two things. Firstly learn about the tactic and how you would use it. Then learn how to respond to the ploy when you see someone using it against you, both of these are equally important.

No Authority Strategy

The No Authority Strategy is really one of these things that the Choleric will find particularly difficult to use. The Choleric doesn't like this. It is a very common mistake made by new salesmen. The new salesman will be in the office a few days, a few weeks, or a few months before turning around and saying, "Hey Boss – I'm losing loads of business. I don't have the authority to give them the discounts and terms that they want. How about you give me more authority to do this?" The new salesman will ask for that authority. The good Sales Manager will say "No, No, No, No, No, No, No!"

It is incredibly hard for the Choleric to accept this. When you are going into a negotiation, the worst possible situation you can have against you, is a vendor who believes that you are the final decision maker, and can agree to anything. That it is entirely down to you, to say, "Yes" or, "No." There are a lot of people with choleric personalities in Property Investing, many people who like 'Doing the Deal'. I know of investors, who are going in and saying, "Hi, I'm a Property Investor, I would like to help you out. Yes we can do a deal. It is all down to me. I've agreed it and of course the buck stops with me". Saying that is actually costing them money.

Question: When is it easier to say "no" to something?

- When you are 'the man' and you could say, "Yes". But it is also just your decision to say, "No".

OR

- When you are the minion, and you are allowed to go to a certain level, and over that you have to say, "I'm terribly sorry - I'm not allowed to do any more."

Answer: The latter.

Does this work? A classic example was at the beginning of this book; in the supermarket with the basket of groceries and not enough cash. It is not just about UK culture; it is about power. Part of the reason that we don't haggle on a basket of goods is that we know what would happen. The girl would say, "I have to ask the manager," and then PING, the little light would go on, and we would be kept standing there with a growing queue of people standing behind us, all getting impatient until the manager came along only to say "No! You are not allowed to do that." You know that if you made an offer to someone like that, it will not be within their remit to accept it.

That is half the reason why you don't. If you thought that you could offer £20 for £25 worth of food with a 50/50 percent chance that the guy on the till might just say, "Yeah, go on then," you would be more tempted to do it.

Large companies do this all the time. They set up layers of managers and structure, with many signature and authority levels. For the precise reason that the person, dealing face to face with the customer at the point of sale, does not have the authority to give anything away on price, or not more than a few percent. You have to go up the sales chain, sales manager to sales director, to get more and more authority. Why? To make it hard. To make it harder for the customers to take advantage of any bargaining power.

The Choleric is going to hate this, as they are going to have to go in there and say, "Well, I represent a group of Property Investors, and as they have asked me to come and look at this property, I'm going to take their instruction. I will put your offer through to them." A Choleric, who gets a big kick out of being 'the man', being 'the big cheese' who can make all the decisions, will find this a big and difficult challenge. The Phlegmatic, incidentally, is absolutely fine with this, they don't have a problem with it at all. The Melancholy also like these nice little ring fenced authority level situations.

Nine times out of ten, when you have a Phlegmatic doing the negotiation, it is because there is a Choleric telling them that that is what they are good at and that is what they should be doing. But I bet you, that when he comes back out of a negotiation, the Choleric is saying, "Why haven't you ..." or "Have you ..." or "Couldn't you do this instead ...."

The lucky thing is that, while saying that to another Choleric would make them really, really affronted;"Why are you telling me how to do my job?", a Phlegmatic would sit there letting it simply wash all over him. He knows that that is the way you are. He knows that he is good at his job. He will get the negotiation done and he will either get the good price or he won't. If he doesn't then it was never going to be possible.

All this ranting and raving that the Choleric is doing is not affecting him in the slightest. That is not an excuse to nag your partner, however, don't be too worried about it as the Phlegmatic is used to it.

Banks use this tactic all the time; they project the idea that there is someone else to go to. Banks call it the “Loan Committee”. Have you noticed that whoever you speak to cannot authorise it, it will have to go to the “Underwriting Committee” or the “Loan Committee”.

Do you know why it is a committee? Because you can't say, “Well then let's go and talk to him.” Do you know what the average Loan Committee looks like in the average UK Bank? It looks like this: “The Computer says 'No'.”

But if the loan person, the salesman, the banker, the teller were to say, “Look I can't do this without authorisation from the Vice President.” You would say, “Okay. Where is her office? Lets go and speak to her now.” But if it is a committee, then suddenly it is not just one person that you can go and talk to. Secondly, there would also be a good reason why that committee would not be available there and then, because a committee which only meets every so often, wouldn't necessarily be in session at that time.

Many of the long time investors that I know either have a partner they work as part of a team, be that a husband and wife, couple or some other team. Many single ones, once the bidding ensues, invent a partner. At a talk I gave once, one guy just burst out laughing, saying,

"I have an imaginary Building Surveyor. I never agree to anything until my Building Surveyor has looked at it."

Even if you are the person with the authority, it is worth giving the impression that you have others to consult. It manages to defuse negotiations from being too confrontational, and gives you an extra delaying tactic (which I'll explain later.)

Frame The Negotiation.

You should know this one: 'Frame the Negotiation' would be the academic way of saying it. What it actually means is 'make a low offer', don't offer the Asking Price. Make an offer which is lower than they expect. Make an offer that is not just a few percent below their asking price.

This is perfectly normal. I know that people who are buying directly from vendors are more typically used to making offers of 20% below the asking price. People have raised the question, "When I put an offer in to an Estate Agent of 20% below the asking price they make me feel really uncomfortable. They make me feel that I shouldn't do it." I will have more later, on why they do it and how to respond to it.

An Example

I sold a flat last October, the first two offers I received were 17% and 20% below the asking price. Making low offers is not unusual. It is expected. It is something that, having sold a few properties in the last few years, I am used to receiving; even when selling through good Estate Agents.

Don't think that you are doing anything unusual just because it is perhaps not what you are used to doing. I guess that maybe some of you are still uncomfortable making what, perhaps in a couple of years time, you won't perceive to be insultingly low offers. You just need to get over it.

Response to "Frame the Negotiation"

With all these ploys there is always a way to respond. What happens when you are selling something and you get a low offer? What happens if you are buying something and they have a very high counter offer? The asking price is framing the negotiation at the top end; if you believe it to be too high, it is the equivalent to making a low offer.

The first thing to remember is that normally the very low offer will be the very first offer made by the purchaser. Generally, once that offer is made, the offer won't go gradually down, it will only increase, before reaching an agreement. Consciously you have to realise that most of the time, low offers aren't there because that is what will be paid, but are there to try and shake the vendor up, putting them on a back foot. There are many people out there who deliberately make low offers for no reason other than to shake up the vendor, trying to break their mindset about what the property is worth.

The Flinch & <Gasp>

But, unconsciously, there is something you need to be able to do; remember what I said about needing to learn some automatic skills?

Here is one of them. When you hear a price that you don't like – NO SCRAP THAT – when you hear a price, ANY price, you have got to flinch. You have got to flinch visibly, or you have got to gasp audibly over the phone. You have got to do everything that you can to make the other person feel uncomfortable, that you do not like their figure.

This is what you are going to practice.

At my seminars I explain that I am about to try and sell them something. Now the price I ask is probably a little more than they are likely to want to pay. I do however point out that, if anyone is stupid enough to agree to my asking price, I have witnesses in the room. The purpose of this set-up is not to try and rip them off by asking far, far too much, it is to get them practising the Flinch and <Gasp>. It has got to be practiced so often that it becomes automatic.

> On my courses, I'll make the offer to those assembled, trying to sell something at an "outrageous price"
>
> "My drinking glass, and it is not just any old drinking glass, but the one I am using at this moment, exclusively filled with the local tap water, with maybe a hint of lemon for flavour." Remember, the longer that they leave it, the lower the water level gets as I take a drink; so the quicker they agree to the deal the more they are going to get. ... "This glass with the water is available to them for ... ONLY ... £169.00. "
>
> <GASP>

They are very good at flinching when I offer them something £168 more than it is worth. But I suspect most are probably fairly bad at flinching when someone is offering them a property at £20,000 more than it is worth. Which would you rather do, pay twenty grand too much for something or £168 too much for something?

I feel so strongly about this that I think you should do a practical. I have done these before and you are going to find it amusing, you are going to find it funny. That is great because anything that helps you remember it, helps it to stick in your mind, will be worthwhile.

So I need you to find a partner for this practical. I want you to ask your partner to read the items I have for sale in the appendix. Then ask them to sell you them, with the full razzmatazz, and build up, and big cheer at the price. The purpose is for you to practice going ... what is the sound? ... For you to practice the gasp and not to agree to the ludicrous prices. Just get that flinch and gasp going.

TIMEOUT for Flinch & <Gasp> practice.

It's worth practising this with a partner. There are, in the appendices, a list of things you might like to try to sell.

You have got to do this, you have got to do this so often that it is so automatic that you don't know how not to. Part of the reason I talk about the Flinch and <Gasp> is that most of the time you will be negotiating over the phone; obviously a flinch won't have the same impact.

We have all heard the alleged statistics: 55% of the impression you get is from how I stand and my gestures, 38% is the tonality of my voice, only 7% is from the actual words used[2].

2 Based loosely on research by Mehrabian and Ferris in 1967, these statistics are the result of one particular experiment and never intended to be generally applied. Whatever the actual numbers, there is general agreement that all modalities are important.

When speaking quickly you appeal more to the sanguine and the choleric types, speaking more slowly you appeal to the phlegmatic type. On the phone you only have the 45% that is audible to go on so you have to make sure that it has all the impact you can muster. You have to make sure that you come up with some noise that is automatic, and is you.

For example those with an American accent might use the words, "You have got to be kidding me,"[3] in a surprised tone. Anything which the other party will think is straight from the gut and think, "my goodness she has reacted badly" - so long as it conveys to the other party how surprised you are by the price.

You have got to flinch whenever an Estate Agent mentions a figure. You have got to flinch whenever a vendor mentions a figure. BUT if you are only doing it with property, it means that it won't be automatic enough. You have got to learn to flinch at car salesmen. You have got to learn to flinch at the checkout price in the supermarket. You have got to flinch at the monitor when you are shopping at amazon.co.uk.

Do this at websites to practice the reflex. Has Amazon ever taken a penny off my shopping cart total because I have flinched at the monitor? NO. Has getting so good at flinching at prices saved me tens to hundreds of thousand pounds over the last ten years? Yes, absolutely! It has got to be so automatic that it happens every time otherwise it is not worth doing at all.

3 You know who you are!

At the end of a talk I was doing, in the bar afterwards, someone mentioned a price for something, and I was talking straight to him. Another person turned round and said "You didn't flinch! I didn't hear you <Gasp>." Others standing around, burst out laughing, and said, "You should have seen his eyes, he did." Everyone knew it.

If it comes over as: "£180,000" then there is a *{pause}* then <Gasp>. Oh! yeah Mark Harrison's course told me I should flinch. It is not good enough; it has got to be an immediate response, straight back. More like; "One hundred and eighty"<Gasp>. Don't even let them finish, you have got to be that fast. It starts with a hundred and eighty, you know that the price is not good enough, you were expecting it to start with "One hundred and sixty" so it doesn't matter if the next figure was a five or a nine.

Seriously, psychologically, the impact it has on the people giving you the price is incredible. I don't think that you will believe it until you have tried it. I think that as you use it you will start to understand how powerful it is, for something so quick and simple.

Response to the Flinch & <Gasp>.

The response, when someone gasps or flinches in response to you, is just to laugh or smile. I find it absolutely hilarious when people try the Flinch or <Gasp> on me, because I know exactly what they are doing. I respect them, but I find myself smiling, or laughing back at them (maybe don't laugh too loudly, it might upset them) and inside I am thinking, "Yeah, Yeah, Yeah." Since running my seminars I have found that people come up to me at events now and deliberately Flinch and <Gasp> at whatever I say. This is great, as it helps me practice how to respond to it.

Being the flinch guy is absolutely fantastic because, if I fail to do it, everyone goes – now hang on a minute. And when they do it back to me, it means that I am getting the practice to make my response automatic. I get to win both ways with this.

Time Tactics

Once you have flinched – and it has got to be your first reaction to any price that you hear mentioned (whether that is the asking price - or they've asked, you've offered and they have come back with another offer) you have got to flinch - then what you must NOT do, under any circumstances, is increase your offer.

Remember what I was saying about getting them to invest time? What you need is a reason why you are not going to increase your offer there and then. That you are going to go away and come back to them later, with an alternative offer.

If they have just come down in price, if you offered £140K, and they have come down, and you straight away over the phone say, "Well maybe I can go to £145K." This gives the impression that you were obviously just haggling. You don't want to come over as someone who is just haggling. You want to come over as someone who is genuinely trying to work with them, and help them by trying to do the best you can. There may be a good reason why you can't come up any more, or much further, so you need some time tactics. It gives the impression that you are serious, that you are professional, that you are on their side and not just trying it on.

There are four time tactics which can be used, by you, or against you. I have included details on each, and how to respond to each so that you are aware of them and know how to react to them.

1. Re-Run the Figures.
2. "You will have to do better than that".
3. Ask the Wife.
4. Other Opportunities.

Time Tactic 1: Re-Run The Figures.

The first time tactic is "I need to re-run the figures." They have named a price. You have gone <GASP>. Then you say, "Tell you what, let me go and re-run my figures."

You do NOT under any circumstances re-run or re-calculate the figures. If you find yourself in any way tempted to re-run the figures, that means that your emotions have started becoming involved. Remember what I said about working out what you can pay, writing it down in big letters, circling it – making sure that it is hard wired into your mind. The only way you re-run the figures is to pick up that piece of paper and read that figure again.

You are not actually doing anything at all. The only reason you are saying, "Let me re-run the figures," is that it buys you time. It leaves the other party, wondering what the next step is. At the moment that you utter the words, "Let me re-run the figures," you know your game plan. The only decision you have to make is how long do I leave it before I call them back with my next move. You should already know that.

Re-running the figures is just taking another look at the figure you have written down. What I do is go swimming, take the children out, watch some television; anything to pass the time before I call back.

When you are in a face-to-face negotiation, carry a pocket calculator. This is not specifically property negotiation, but when I used to do commercial contracts, for employers and subsequently clients, I would say, "I need to re-run the figures, I need some space to use. Do you have a room I can sit down in for five minutes just on my own?" and I would walk out of the room. I would never do it in front of them.

Certainly use this when dealing directly with vendors, perhaps suggesting "Let me sit out in the car and see if there is something better I can do." Pretend to calculate something, but again re-read the written down figure.

Response to "Re-run the figures"

Firstly you smile, but basically you are gracious, you realise that it is a ploy, you have to appreciate that it is nothing more than that.

Actually if you can encourage them to really do it and let their emotions take charge of them, great! But just be gracious, and give the impression that you are not desperate. Say, "Certainly, how long do you think you will need? ... So I can expect to hear back from you in an hour/the morning, absolutely no problem. Give me a call when you are ready."

Never give the impression that you are desperate; the Choleric can come over as a desperate person. They are so keen to get the deal done, to get another tick in the "number of properties" box.

Again, spend your time doing something completely unrelated, go swimming etc. Do something so that you are not tempted to call.

Time Tactic 2: "You'll Have To Do Better Than That"

There is another tactic, another delaying tactic, but it is also more, it is even better than that. These are probably the most valuable words you will ever use.

So you have made an offer, and they have come back with a counter offer, they name the figure and you <GASP>. Quite often it is worth following up with saying, "Tch! No, you are going to have to do better than that." (or if through an Estate Agent, "No, I'm sorry they will have to do better than that.")

Quite often that is all you will need to say, and you will find that they will come back inside an hour or two with possibly another five to ten grand. No concessions on your part, just a time tactic.

It is a bit like a tennis match. You both knock the ball alternatively. When the ball is in your court, you can hold onto it making the other party wait for your next move. However, if either party makes a move without the ball, i.e. out of turn, rather than waiting to receive a response; it indicates how desperate, how needy, they are. That party is now on the back foot.

How you view this tactic depends on your point of view – some people have found it so valuable, that they call this "The Seven Magic Words". Others have found it so old and dated that they call it "Noah's Ark" (because it's so old that Noah took two of them with him!)[4]

4 See "Essential Negotiation" by Gavin Kennedy, published by The Economist, p. 136

I've found that in commercial negotiation, it's regarded like Noah, but when buying property, it can be worth several hundred pounds per word.

Response to "You will have to do better than that".

The only response to this, is to smile and say, "Let me think!".

The ball is now in your court as, once they have asked you to do better, you can quickly turn this around and make it your time tactic. Again you have control of the time. It is up to you when you will go back to them, and they are the ones worrying about when you will.

Time Tactic 3: Ask The Wife

This is the version I use. Now I can understand why ladies, you might need to change the wording slightly. For those of you without a wife, lets make it obvious; you can use: Ask the Husband / Boyfriend/ (or more increasingly these days a good term is) Partner.

Which you use depends on how you want to appear: the professional investor, or as the nice guy, the nice girl, the nice couple, whoever you want to be buying the house. If you want to come over as the nice guy then you are certainly able to get away with, "Let me go and ask the wife, I will have a talk to her." Giving the impression that you are trying to get on the housing ladder, and are possibly very constrained in how much you have to spend, is sometimes the right way to go.

Other times coming over as the professional investor, saying, "Let me ask my partner, we have a set of formulae to work out how much we can afford to pay, otherwise it doesn't stack up with our business model," is sometimes the way to go. But having both techniques in your armoury, and with intuition knowing when to use one or the other, can prove to be useful upon occasions.

If you need to, you can then arrange another viewing with your "partner". I have been known to take my mother-in-law to second viewings. My mother-in-law is now in her late seventies. Her father was, himself, a property developer back in the late forties and fifties. She was brought up going round houses, she loves looking at houses built in the last fifty years to see how architectures have evolved. It is not what she says as she is going round, she is very good as she goes round staying absolutely silent. But picture it, here I am with this seventy plus old lady – what conclusion do you think the vendors are drawing from this, when I go round with her? - "Ooh, she is probably lending him the money." "She is probably putting some money down on this."

Excellent! The less power I seem to have, the less they can get upset when I am unable to come up to their price. Because now it is very clear that there are other people involved in the deal. This "Ask your partner" is a fantastic double whammy; it is a time tactic that buys you time to get their emotions to work against them, and it reduces your perceived power.

The less perceived power you have, the nicer they tend to be with you, and generally the more accommodating they are. Remember the new salesman when you are doing this; the new salesman always says, "I have got the power to do this." The good sales manager says, "No you haven't. You have got to ask me."

Again the Choleric will find it difficult. The strong Choleric, particularly a strong choleric male, will find it very difficult, if he has to say, "I have to go and ask the girlfriend if it is Okay to spend this amount of money to buy a house." Would you rather have the reputation of being a Big Strong Choleric Bloke or be the guy who shaves an extra five grand off each property deal he makes?

Response to "Ask the wife".

The first thing that you do with all these tactics is smile. If someone says, "I need to go to speak to the wife," reply, "That is absolutely great, I am glad." and then possibly add, "If you want, I can come along and meet with them. To explain anything directly with them." Ask them to set a time, push them for a time, "When are you going to speak to him" / "When are you going to speak to her?" ... "in that case shall I call ...?"

If you can, particularly if it is a business partner, try and get their commitment that when they ask their partner they will be making a recommendation.

If the Investor comes along and says, "Look I am representing a group of investors, and I don't know whether they are prepared to pay this." As the vendor I can say, "They normally take your recommendation don't they?" If the Investor is not good at suppressing his own ego, the chances are he will say, "Yeah," particularly if there is no partner and they have invented them for the sake of the negotiation ploy.

This will either flush out the non-existence of the partner, get them to agree to discuss a recommendation for the deal, or it flushes out an objection. If the investor says, "Well, I don't think I am going to be able to recommend it because I don't think the price is right," then suddenly, there is no time advantage on his side. It has just given me the opening I need to try to get more money out of him.

The response has two steps, to offer to help or to ask if the person is going to give a recommendation, and then to act accordingly.

Time Tactic 4: Other Opportunities

The final time tactic is, "I am looking at other things, I have got other opportunities". Obviously this works particularly well if you have come over as an investor. It should work equally well if you have come over as a first time buyer or someone looking for a bigger family home. It indicates once again that you don't need them as much as they need you. If they need you they will respond to it. If they don't need you, this time tactic won't work – but then again if they didn't need you, you were never going to get the great price, the 'below market deal', anyway.

It is that "Is It True or Not" again.

Response to "Other opportunities".

If they have other opportunities, you can generally disarm them by smiling and saying, "Yes of course." Don't make it one sided.

If you have ever bought or sold a property through an Estate Agent, the agent uses the 'Other Opportunities' tactic all the time. If you are buying, they always tell you that there are other interested purchasers, don't they? "Had three viewings this weekend and we are expecting another offer this evening."

It is a fantastic chance to call the tactic, and find out whether it is true. If an Estate Agent says this to me, I respond saying, "Well I don't want to get into a bidding war. It is probably more sensible if you let the other offer go ahead, but obviously if the other buyer does drop out then give me a call and I will see what I can offer then."

It is amazing how many other offers drop out within a couple of hours just as a result of saying that. It is amazing how many of those other buyers turn out to be entirely imaginary. Remember that the 'other buyers' is just another guise of the 'Other Opportunities' tactic used on you.

As I said before, negotiation is only part of the process. It is also a way to filter the really good deals. Negotiation includes a lot of deal filtering to go through before actual purchasing.

If there are no other opportunities for you to move on to, then remember your BATNA. Not investing in a deal can always be seen as your 'other opportunity' if you have already filtered out any other potential deals.

How Much Time?

The amount of time you allow before getting back to the vendor all depends on the vendor's known circumstances. If the vendor has already indicated that they are really up against a wall and they need a decision in the next day, then clearly I have to say I will be back to them within the hour. I may take ninety minutes. However, if the vendor is not giving that impression then of course I will say that I will get back to them in the morning. I might leave it to lunchtime.

To clarify, I have found that the delay has been more effective than closing the deal there and then. Remember that I am predominately making offers via the Estate Agents, so am not dealing with the vendors direct. However, by the time that you have got to the stage of meeting the vendor face to face, you would first have had a couple of phone calls, with perhaps some offers going back and forth. So the positions have already moved, and you would be closer to finalising things.

Small Increments

When you come back with any new offer you should only change your figure by a small amount.

If you come back changing the price by a big amount, the psychology you will set up in the mind of the other party, is that of, “Ooh! He just came up with another ten grand – he must have another five grand more available.” If on the other hand, you were only to have offered another five hundred, they are unlikely to think that there is much more available.

Of course, if the best offer your opponent is making is already within your acceptable range, then be very careful with this one – you don't want to lose a good deal by being too greedy.

I sold a house about eighteen months ago. I thought that I should get £175k-£177k for it. I spoke to the Estate Agent and he thought that was reasonable, We agreed to put the property on the market for £179,900.

Within a couple of days I had a viewing from a couple of young guys who wanted to buy the house to jointly to get their feet on the property ladder. They made an offer. Mike, my Estate Agent said, "They are offering One Hundred and Seventy". <GASP> I then said, "It is not going to happen Mike, they are going to have to do better than that."

That afternoon they came back with another offer of £175,000.

After my immediate <GASP> I expressed my dissatisfaction with this offer and said, "Let me talk to Mary about it. I will give you a call back in the morning, Mike."

In the morning, when I called Mike back I said, "Well Mike, we have talked it over and we can only come down by a couple of hundred quid. We can only reduce the price from £179,900 to £179,700." Mike said that he would see what they thought.

Two hours later Mike came back and said, "You will like this one Mark – they have offered £179,700."So in the space of two days I had come down two hundred pounds, and they had come up by nine thousand seven hundred.

A lot of that was just the basics; going through an Estate Agent, saying, "They need to do better than that," then only coming down by a tiny amount. In that case it worked really well. Remember with property, as an investor, negotiation is all about filtering. The ones that get away don't matter, provided that there are enough that don't.

Had I come down by two and a half thousand then they would probably have thought that "having come down two and a half grand he must have another grand in it."

Now consider the mistake they made: they had come up five thousand pounds. I was immediately thinking, they could have another two to three grand, I wasn't expecting it – indeed I was a little shocked when they accepted my £179,700 figure. I would have sold it for £177,000! But if someone offers me another two thousand seven hundred for doing absolutely nothing, of course I am going to accept it.

Also, if I hadn't come down at all, they might have fallen for it. But more likely, they might have just thought that I was a stick in the mud, and no agreement would have been reached. So, coming down a couple of hundred pounds, even though the two figures were nearly five grand apart, gave the impression that I was really trying. I had made a concession.

Concessions

Generally, perhaps not when there is only a couple of hundred quid in it, but certainly when making any bigger concessions, then there needs to be a condition attached to it. It is not as if I have been haggling and I have suddenly 'through magic' found another five grand in the pot. Try to avoid the "Through magic I have found another five grand in the pot"; it is important to have a plausible reason for the increase.

This is another reason to have, or to invent, a partner. It can be very useful as it allows you in good faith, to put in a low offer. The partner can, upon reflection, decide that they can afford a further five grand and ask you to convey this.

The alternative is to attach conditions to any big change in your offer. Always ask for something, even if you don't always get it. Maybe you ask for the curtains to be included, maybe say, "Well look, I can offer the other four thousand you are looking for but you will need to leave the fridge, the washing machine, the dishwasher and the oven in there."

Even if they were going to do that anyway, it is making them feel better. They have wrung that out of you, it wasn't just you giving it away. They have had to give something back and they will be pleased with themselves because they have got another four grand out of you just for leaving the appliances there; and they were going to do that anyway. Absolutely brilliant, not only have you got the price you were looking for, but you have left them thinking that they have got a really fantastic deal as they had been so smart. Isn't that exactly what you want?

If it doesn't work and they say no to the condition, respond that you are looking at other opportunities, or another ploy (which I will come to and explain later). Leave it a day, and see what they say. If they stick their feet in the mud, and they don't come back to you, then it means that they were never sufficiently motivated anyway. If they are motivated then they are going to come back to you and say, "Well look, maybe we can come to some agreement".

But concessions need concessions, it can be something that really doesn't matter at all like, maybe, a change in date. Try, "If we were to offer you another grand, would it be possible for you to exchange a month later? We have got some other things coming through which will free up some extra cash. We can offer you that extra thousand, but we would need to exchange a month later."

Obviously you will only be offering the higher price if it is profitable anyway; if the price still makes sense to you. But making them feel that the only reason that you offered them extra money is because they themselves conceded something, is about getting them to feel that they have won the negotiation, so that they are not going to back out in the time between agreement and exchange.

Splitting The Difference (And Losing)

This brings me then to another ploy commonly used by the amateur. Most people will understand the term 'Splitting the Difference'. Have you ever offered to 'split the difference'?

I certainly hope not – because whoever **OFFERS** to split the difference **LOSES**. But what you are trying to do is to encourage the other party to offer to split the difference. The reason why people offer to split the difference is because they think it is fair.

Your neighbour selling his lawnmower for a hundred quid, you might offer eighty, then you agree to split the difference – well fair enough. The figures involved are negligible in the general scheme of things, so in that instance, splitting the difference is okay (and your ongoing relationship with your neighbour is also important.). But in property negotiation, the sums of money are far greater.

Let's think about whether it is fair or not. There you are as the investor, and have made hopefully an initial offer that is deliberately low because you are trying to shake them up. As on average, people move house every seven years, the vendor has no real idea what house prices are doing. The vendor only has what they have been told down the pub by their mate, or what they read in the local papers, or what their Estate Agent has told them.

They have gone to three Estate Agents, who have each given a different figure. The first has said, "Well, it is worth £170,000." The next has said, "No, we can sell it for more than that, we can sell it for

£175,000." The third Estate Agent says, "I don't know why they think that they can only sell it for £175,000. We can definitely sell it for £180,000 Sir." Ca-ching! They have landed the client and are now listing the property for £180,000.

They have been reeled in hook, line and sinker. They have gone to the Estate Agent who has claimed they can sell it for the most money. The Estate Agent has made up a price for the sole purpose of getting them to sign an exclusive contract with that agency. You have offered a low price to try and shake them up a bit and somehow the middle of those two numbers is FAIRNESS? That the average of two made up numbers is fair? That it is justice? How did that work out?

Even if you still believe that it is fair, after that scorn and derision on my part, let me ask you the following question: why are you investing in property? Is it to make money for you and your children, or is it to increase the amount of perceived justice in the world?

You should encourage the other party to offer to split the difference and then you treat that as a new offer.

Remember the property I was selling for just shy of £180,000, they were offering £170,000 when they split the difference by offering £175,000. What did I do? <GASP> and then treated it as a new offer. I treated it just as I would any other offer. Just because the new offer happens to be mid-way between the two original figures, doesn't make it any different. I know people who have got the vendors to split the difference three times. They might start £10,000 apart. The vendor offers to split the difference repeatedly, and end up £1,200 apart.

Splitting the difference - you should work with it if, and only if, the other party does it. If you do it and you are up against an experienced negotiator, then you have just caused yourself a real problem. The experienced negotiator will treat it as a new offer. From 10,000 apart you have just came up 5,000, they will think that you wouldn't have done that unless you had another 2,500 or so in the pot. They will know, if you came up from 170,000 to 175,000, that they have got you landed on at least 177,000, and maybe a bit higher.

So 'splitting the difference' – please, please don't do it, but try to get the other party to do it. Doing that can work out terribly well for you.

Good Cop, Bad Cop

'Splitting the difference' is one of the favoured ploys of the man in the street. The other is 'Good Cop, Bad Cop'. We are all familiar with 'Good Cop, Bad Cop' as seen in any American movie.

Bad Cop in gruff voice:	“Yeah if you don’t agree to this - things are going to be really difficult for you.”
Good Cop to suspect:	“Oh isn't he so horrible!”
Good Cop to Bad Cop:	“Why don’t you go out and have a coffee. I will see if I can talk to him.”
Good Cop to Suspect in Camp Voice:	“Now that he is out of the room, wasn’t he nasty to you? Well I will help you, give me something here, and I will make sure that he...”

Well okay, we may have never seen an American movie quite that poorly written. But the point is, we all understand the idea of 'Good Cop, Bad Cop' and we come across it all the time. I cannot think of a single property purchase through an Estate Agent, where this hasn’t reared its head at some point.

Estate Agents use 'Good Cop, Bad Cop' all the time. They regularly say things like, “I have suggested to my vendor that they accept your offer but they are holding out for a higher price and there is nothing I can do." The Estate Agent is trying to make out that he, the Estate Agent, is Good Cop, and the vendor is Bad Cop. Er No!

There is no Good Cop! The vendor is Bad Cop! The Estate Agent is Worse Cop! It really is that simple.

If there is no Estate Agent involved, that is what the partner was invented for. If a partner is used, then the person you are dealing with is always the Good Cop, and their partner is always Bad Cop. It can get terribly humorous if you are watching out for it.

If there genuinely is a Bad Cop partner, or if an Estate Agent does this, and you get the feeling that they are experienced negotiators, then sometimes you can just laugh and say, "You are not trying to do 'Good Cop, Bad Cop' on me are you?"

I don't do it so much in property negotiation, but I do so more often in Commercial Negotiation.

The most important thing is not to fall for it, but to realise that a lot of the time it is a negotiation ploy, not a statement of fact. It's important to be able to differentiate fact from fiction, particularly when you are up against someone who knows how to negotiate.

The Estate Agent can be turned into Good Cop using 'The Subversion' technique outlined in the Advanced Negotiation Ploys section, more of that later.

Silence

On my training courses, at this point, I will start to say a sentence and then stop mid-way through.

I will say:

- You need to remember to make a low...
- After you make a new offer, you should go...

Without fail, someone in the room will complete my sentence for me.

Why do you use silence in a negotiation? Because you want to make them uncomfortable.

This is quite humorous when it happens in a training course, but absolutely fantastic when you do it with the Estate Agent and they blurt out something like, “Look, they are going to go for a couple of grand less, when I go back and talk to them, but they will agree to it.” Sometimes people blurt out something that they shouldn’t have done just because you shut up and listened.

Anyone who has had any good sales tactics training will know that a good salesperson will aim to listen for two thirds of the meeting, and talk for one third of the meeting. Whether you call it a sales technique, a negotiation technique, a communication technique, or a rapport building technique, call it what you will. It is there. It works. Understand when to talk and when to be quiet.

Response to "Silence".

How do you respond to silence?

.... with more silence.

If someone is trying the silence ploy on you just be quiet. If you ever want a really good laugh, try watching two good "salespersons" trying to sell something to each other, because sometimes you get a silence deadlock when both are trying the silence ploy, and they will sit there for five or six minutes until one of them talks when their nerve breaks.

The only way to respond to silence is to be silent. Do not feel the need to jump in and fill any break in the conversation with noise. This is another reason why the Phlegmatic is so good at negotiation. Typically, the Phlegmatic is very comfortable with silence. I'm not phlegmatic, I find it very difficult to keep silent. I want to talk when there is a gap. As a choleric I find it very hard to be silent - giving away the power is hard for us but understand you are not relinquishing any power by being silent. The Sanguine, you are just going to plain hate it.

Non Round Number

When you get to your final offer, don't make it a round number. Round numbers are big signals that maybe you can go a little further. If you go back with a non-round number, people believe that you have spent a lot of time working out exactly what your final figure can be.

I was talking to the Group Commercial Director of a FTSE100 company, and asking him, "Why do you price items at £4.99, instead of £5.00? Does anyone fall for the lower price, about making a big saving of a penny?" His answer was rather more sophisticated than that:

It turns out that if they price a product at exactly £5.00 then many customers think, "Well the price should really be £4.70. They have rounded up the price to a whole number." However, when the price is a non-round number customers tend not to go through that mental thought process, and don't question how that price has been arrived at. It is all about the price being an non-round number, not the extra revenue generated. Research has found that although a penny in revenue is given away, many more sale conversions are gained as a result. When people see a round number the temptation is to question it.

Just the same is true with property negotiation; make your final offer a non-round number, £179,700, not £179,500 or £180,000. Certainly if you look on the Internet, at information products they tend to end in a seven, thirty seven, fifty seven, ninety seven etc.

Negotiation Ploys

In property negotiation, you should always spend an extra phone call making a fuss about the last £100 in a price. Not because the £100 is material in any way, but because it reinforces the impression in the mind of the vendor that they have made you work hard, and gotten themselves the very best price you had to offer.

The Final Offer

There is one phrase you need to be careful with, and that is the phrase “that's my final offer”.

If you say this, and then go back later with a higher offer,then your Estate Agent knows that you will beat your 'final offer' next time as well.

When you get to your best price, then you should make it clear that this is the final offer, and that if it's not accepted, then the negotiation is over and the outcome is no deal.

The best way to signal a final offer, is to use a very, very, small change in price, as well as a phrase like “that's my best offer”.

Leave The Door Open.

The whole final gambit ploy is an example of where the Estate Agent can help with your reputation. The thing that you have to be careful about with the Final Gambit is that you don't make it utterly final. You generally start with, "Look that is my final offer, and I really need to know by the end of the week." Or if you haven't set a time and you haven't heard, you phone back after a few days. "Look, just to let you know, I am going to need a decision by Friday as there are other things that I am looking at. I need to know if this one is going ahead or if I can re-allocate my capital."

The ball is in their court. Never be afraid to give them longer time-scales then you think they will need because that is when their emotions work for you. But you have got to leave the door open, set a time limit and if the time runs out, say, "Okay, Fair enough. Clearly they think that they are going to get a better offer, don't they? If things change, and it is another few weeks and they haven't, by all means give me a bell and I will see if I am in a position to proceed."

You have got to leave the door sort of ajar, where there is no commitment on your part that you will proceed if they phone back to you in a month's time. But equally they now feel that it will definitely be worth their time making you that phone call to see whether you might. You never know when you might get a phone call out of the blue, six or eight weeks later from someone who did have time on their side but has used those six to eight weeks to turn themselves into a desperate vendor. Generally when this happens it is because they have found their dream house, and being put under pressure with, "You must get a sale agreement on you own house or we are not going to accept your offer!" and they could now lose this house they have fallen in love with.

I have bought some properties this way from people who have fallen in love with another property and have left it too long, because they had got too greedy selling their house. People who have had offers which they didn't accept as they thought that they could do better, and now are forced to accept something far, far lower.

I bought a house just down the road from me. I only discovered the facts about six months later.

The property was on the market for £178,000. I thought that a fair Market Value was around the £175,000 figure. The agent had, it turned out, advised the vendor to put it on at £175,000, but he had said, "No it is a rising market,

It had been on the market for two days, at £178,000 and he had an offer of £175,000, which he turned down. He through that if he had got such an offer within two days, he'd be bound to get the asking price within a couple of weeks. Eight weeks later he has put an offer in another house,, which has been accepted. He was coming under a lot of pressure to get his sold or he wouldn't be able to complete.

I got a call out of the blue, from the Estate Agent, asking me to come and put one of my "silly low offers" in. The Estate Agent didn't think I would get the property, saying, "He is asking too much but I don't want to lose the listing. I think he should be asking £175,000 come and make one of your silly offers, help me shock him, and then maybe he will re-list at £175,000. Because at £175,000 we can get a lot of viewings next week."

So I offered £160,000, not stupidly low, and agreed £165,000 the following day.

It wasn't me who had made that £175,000 offer. But had it been me who had made the earlier offer, do you think it would have been sensible for me to say, "Well if there is an issue and things change come back to me"?

Had he been able to do that, he would have been a lot better off. Having made an offer I try very hard to keep the offer open and if things do change for them – then by all means they can come back and maybe we can pick up a few weeks later.

The only time this doesn't work is in a fast tumbling market. That is why I say, you have got to keep the door ajar, but, with no commitment. It is: IF things change give me a bell and we will see IF there is anything we can do.

Advanced Negotiation Ploys – Or Dirty Tactics

I am going to start off with some of the dirty tricks, or the things that I consider to be dirty tricks. I am not advocating that you use any of these but that you can recognise when the technique is being used against you.

The Subversion

For a while I played around with what I should call this. At first I wanted to call it the seduction, but then I realised that no one would ever fall for my suggestion that they should seduce an Estate Agent. So I decided that subversion was a better description for this technique.

The thing about Estate Agents is that, in principle, they are on the vendor's side. In principle the Estate Agent is there to get the best deal possible. Note that I said the best DEAL not the best price. The good Estate Agents also understands the money, speed, and security triangle as well, and try to get what suits their clients. In practice it may not always work that way.

Trying to pin this down could be difficult but fortunately there has been some research done by an American University which has looked into this. A book I would strongly recommend is a book called

Freakonomics [5]. It is by a very high powered American Economist, and takes a look at a lot of interesting random things through life. One of those things was a big, big study of American Realtors, and how much they sold houses for. He was able to identify that when Realtors were selling their own houses it took, on average, a week longer to sell, and they got about an extra 2% - which for a typical American house is about $10,000.

It is kind of interesting. You would have thought that the Realtor would have been working really, really hard to get the best price for their client. But what actually happens is, being only human, they get a good price. However, the Realtors are torn between holding out for another $10,000 or closing out the sale now. The Realtor's personal taking is only going to be about $100 for the higher price. So do they risk the sale, when all that is in it for them is $100, or do they close it and secure the commission they have already earned?

However, when they are selling their own home they are balancing the full $10,000 against the loss of the sale - not just a few $100 extra in commission.

In the UK, the way that Estate Agents are typically structured, the figures are even more skewed. We don't have a culture of Independent Realtors, or Franchise Realtors, or have a REMAX system, stuff like that where Estate Agents basically own their businesses. The majority of negotiators are employees. If an Estate Agency is getting 1% of the sale; that means that for an extra £10,000 the company will get an extra £100 in commission. The agency is probably paying their negotiator

5 See Appendix B

2% of that fee as a bonus. Then for every £10,000, the negotiator gets for the vendor, he will get only an extra £2 in his pocket.

Compared to that are things like getting the commission already achieved in the sale and meeting their targets so that they don't lose their job and have to go down the road and start again with a plain Mondeo. (You know how Estate Agents work: Mondeo - promotion - Mondeo GL - promotion - Mondeo GLS?)

Estate Agents can, sometimes, be motivated to get the sale agreed; rather than necessarily get the best price for their client. To use this knowledge against the Estate Agent can be said to be a dirty tactic. At this stage, you are most definitely asking the Estate Agent to do something that is not in their clients best interests. So you are going to need to be very subtle about it.

I mention this so that you are aware of this if you are ever selling properties through an Estate Agent, so you can make sure that this isn't happening to you. Make sure that your Estate Agent isn't getting the sale in the bag when he knows that if left on the market another week, and he spends another four hours showing people around, he would probably get a better offer and get you another couple of thousand pounds. So be very careful that this isn't happening to you.

If you are buying the temptation is to use it when the Estate Agent 'Good Cop, Bad Cops' you. When the Estate Agent is playing the Good Cop saying, "I am going to try and get them to accept your price." then play along with it. Get them to put the offer to their vendor the aim is to get the Estate Agent to spend time convincing the vendor to accept less rather than the purchaser to pay more.

Another thing is when I am selling properties, I sometimes agree a radically different commission structure. I would advise people to do this. When the Estate Agent says that the property will sell for £170,000. Then say to him, "Okay. I will offer you 1% of everything up to that figure plus 10% of anything above that." This is particularly good when you are dealing with Independent Estate Agents, where that commission is actually going straight into their pockets. They know that if they get an extra £10,000 on the price then they are taking home an extra £1,000. This is great for their business.

Typically, when selling through an Estate Agent, you agree commission rates with the agency (the company). This will typically be 1% of the sale price. Incidentally, if you end up paying more than 1% - it means that you haven't negotiated your fees well enough. Estate Agents often say, "Our standard fees are 2% +VAT." I'll reply, "They are your standard fees, but what am I going to pay?" Normally I Pay 1% to 1 ¼%. If I list a property, sole agency, I will pay 1%. I will also go on to say that I own several other properties in the area and if they do a good job for me then, when I come to sell, I will list the rest of them through them. If they have done a good job I commit to that.

Sometimes people are worried that, if the Estate Agent has two similar properties and is going to get 2% on one and only 1% on theirs, then the Estate Agent is going to market the other property more vigorously. This might be the case if I didn't have anything else to offer them, but not when I say, "Look, I own other properties in the area, and I am planning to sell five or six of them over the next couple of years. You will get all this business if you do a good job for me."

1% commission on five or six properties is greater than 2% on only one.

These days, with the transparency of the Land Register, within a couple of months I can tell whether they have done a good job and understand what the prices really were.

It is also about building the personal relationships with the Estate Agents. They have to trust me that I really will do that if, and only if they do a good job. That is all about subverting the Estate Agent.

The "I've Discovered ..." Ploy

This really is a dirty tactic and I have already touched on it earlier. It is a dirty tactic that buyers use more than vendors. It is when you and the other party have agreed a price and then, a week before exchange the vendor gets a phone call to say, "Oh, the survey has come back and there is damp. So clearly we are going to have to re-negotiate our price. I hadn't realised that there was damp."

Sometimes this can genuinely be true. The survey has shown up something that the vendor could not possibly have known. It is reasonable to say, that if it is one of those things that comes up, then so be it.

If, however, you have viewed a property and you discover that there is water flowing down the walls, there is mould all the way round the ceiling, there is mould underneath the carpets and you are trudging through a soggy mess as you walk through the kitchen, and you then have the audacity to phone up a week before exchange to say, "I hadn't realised that there was damp," then it is a dirty trick negotiation tactic.

When someone does this against you, you have got to ask yourself if it really is a surprise, or if it is a tactic.

> I had a big argument with another investor when she and I were on an "experts panel" at a conference at the Savoy last year. One of the audience asked a question which boiled down to "There are obviously damp problems at the property – I knew this from the first viewing - should I turn round and offer a lower price just before exchange?"
>
> The other investor said, "Yes, you should go back and get a lower price".
>
> I said, "No, if the damp was obvious, then you should have built that into the negotiations, and once you'd agreed the price, you should stick by your word."
>
> The other investor said, "I'm a businesswoman – I'd always go back and get the better price."
>
> My reply was that even if you put moral considerations aside (which I can't, by the way) then looked at purely objectively I believe that a reputation for integrity is, in the long run, worth far more to your business than the few thousand here or there achieved you when go back and take advantage of someone.

If I had done that to someone then maybe, this time, I might get an extra couple of thousand off the price on this property! But how is the Estate Agent going to feel, when he comes to recommending me, when he comes to sell me the next one? Or how is that vendor going to feel about being asked to be a referral customer and being a testimonial customer for my business?

How is that vendor going to feel about it? If one of his friends has a problem you want him to refer you with, "Give Mark a call he can help out in your circumstances." You never want to hear, "Never deal with Mark, he will offer you a price and then try to stuff you because he pretends that he hasn't noticed that there is damp." You want "Yeah he came through ..." and so forth.

Generally, if genuinely big things come up at the survey that you couldn't have been expected to know, then fair enough. They have got to be 'Genuine', 'Big' and 'Unknown'. Not just a negotiating ploy that you had planed to discover, although you had known about it all along, and were just going to bring it out once everyone thought they had got an agreement.

Absolutely fine to bring these things up before you have shaken hands and agreed on a price. Where it becomes a dirty trick is when you have reached an agreement, then you pretend to find something that you knew about all along. My view is that once you have agreed a price you have got to stick to it; that is where your reputation lies.

The "I'm Blatantly Evil" Ploy

This ploy is an extreme version of the "I've discovered..." ploy and I call it the "I'm Blatantly Evil" technique. Perhaps my view on ethics is shown here. If you are reading this, you won't get the benefit of the visual clue, a broad smile, as this is genuinely how I respond to this.

The "I'm Blatantly Evil" technique is where the price is agreed and then the day before exchange, or the week before exchange, there is a phone call to say, "No, I've changed my mind, I am only prepared to offer five grand less," or "I need five grand more." This is accompanied with no attempt to justify this move. It is just that, now you are ready to go, I am going to try to push you.

Frankly I don't fall for this. At this stage if someone tries this on me I would rather walk away from the deal; keeping my reputation as someone who can't be pushed over, save and keep my integrity, rather than pay the extra five grand. I also assume that most people who are selling or buying would do the same.

If this happens through an Estate Agent then, quite often, you find that the Estate Agent is terribly uncomfortable about it. The Estate Agent knows that they might make an extra few pounds if the vendor gets away with it but more likely they are in real danger of losing all the commission and then having to spend lots more work trying to get another sale agreed.

If the vendor has done this to this buyer, then the Estate Agent wonders what on earth are they going to do to the next buyer! It quite often backfires when they try it; they then find it much, much harder to get the deal completed as word spreads terribly quickly. This is a case where you can, with a clear conscience, just subvert the Estate Agent.

Often the Estate Agent will agree "I don't think that he should have done this and I will try and help you to get through this." But sometimes you just have to walk away and say, "No. If you are going to up the asking price by five grand. Well it is very simple I am going to say No to that. In fact I am not going to hold you to our original agreement. I am going to offer five grand less than we had agreed on originally. If you are going to do it to me then I am going to do it to you. That is the new offer on the table, are you going to accept it? What do you reckon?"

But in those circumstances, if somebody has tried to use the "I'm Blatantly Evil" tactic, whichever of you it is, then you will find that all trust is gone. It also means that all those little things, which make moving in or out of a property relatively painless, you can broadly expect to disappear.

If you have tried this on a vendor don't expect the property to be in anything like a nice condition when you go to move in. Some vendors vacuum round as the last thing they do before they go because they want to hand over to that nice man who is buying it from them and leave it tidy. You can safely say that they won't do this if you have tried any dirty trick on them. Indeed if there are gentlemen involved, when you go check out the loo, you find that their aim has been poor, or they have left a lot of stuff about the day before they move out.

Dealing With Estate Agents

Now the reason I have put this section in is that over the last few years I have seen the pendulum swing in the property investment community.

Five to ten years ago we were calling ourselves 'Landlords' weren't we? Then we became 'Buy-to-Letters', and now we are 'Property Investors'. Apparently landlords is sounding too Dickensian for the modern young trendy image of the profession.

However, with the change in image came a change of approach. A few years ago everyone was dealing through Estate Agents and then this 'Well actually if you try to find vendors directly, you can target in on the motivated vendors, then you can get much better deals' approach came along. [6]

6 My coming book, due for publication in 2007 goes into far more detail on this "direct" approach.

The problem with the new approach is that over the last three years I have seen far, far more people trying to do it. I can't see any stop to this trend as more people try to find the motivated vendor and get in and try to find the direct sales. That can only mean more and more competition. Irrespective of how good your advertising is, and how efficient your processes are. At the end of the day, if someone is desperate and they look through the local paper, and they find "We buy houses quickly for cash!" they may phone them up. If someone is really desperate and they find four "We buy houses quickly for cash!" adverts, they are likely to phone up all four of them.

Vendors who really need this service are going to go to everyone who advertises. In which case that will create a lot more competition. This means that either the prices are going to be pushed up, or you are going to pay the same prices but you are only going to get a quarter of the business as it is spread around further. I think that gradually this is already happening. People have become obsessive about buying direct because they have seen a small number of people doing very well. People are buying direct to the exclusion of everything else.

So I have written this chapter to remind everyone that actually sometimes Estate Agents do come up with very good deals. Don't for one moment think that I am saying that you should not try to identify the motivated vendor and deal with them directly, build the rapport, or do the things that are getting you the good property deals. What I am saying is that, if that is the only way that you do your business, you may well find yourself getting squeezed. Don't rule out the 90% of houses that are currently sold through Estate Agents. Sometimes good deals can come up through them.

Estate Agents can be very good value to you, providing you remember that actually they are not your agent. The Estate Agent is not there to get you a good deal; they are not there to be fair. The Estate Agent is there to get a good deal for their client, the vendor. They will be useful to you when you are the vendor, so don't discount them.

They can also be useful to you when you are buying, with the credibility issue. Anyone with fifteen pounds to spare, and an evening, can put two hundred flyers through their local doors saying, "We buy properties for cash." Anyone with a couple hundred pounds can get an advert in the Local Property Paper to blanket the area. Anyone with a small amount of money, and a sixteen year old friend can come up with a website.

It is very, very easy. There are no barriers to entry, to saying, "I am a Property Investor and I buy properties for cash," and get big exposure. I know it is easy, I know so many people who have started up buying property this way in the last six months. They are getting a good number of leads coming through and are buying a couple of properties a month now. If the barriers to entry are that low then there is going to be a credibility gap and, sooner or later, bad apples are going to turn up. There are going to be less scrupulous investors who are going to give all the rest of us a bad name.

Comments are going to arise like. "Yeah, my mates were going to sell to one of these investors and the day before exchange they just pulled out. It turns out that they had put offers on too many houses and they didn't have enough cash to buy my mate's house." I am beginning to meet investors who are saying this when they are using these techniques.

I met one guy, an investor, only the other week. He explained, "I have six offers on the table but I only have enough cash to be able to go ahead with four. I am going to pick and chose which ones I am going to go ahead with just before I exchange."

What is that going to do for our reputation as private Property Investors? This is why I think that buying through Estate Agents is coming back into vogue. An Estate Agent putting an offer to the vendor saying, "Yes I know that it is a low offer, but I have dealt with Mr Harrison over the last twelve years and when he says four weeks he means four weeks. He has never backed out of a sale with me." It can be a lot more credible than "Yeah I'm Dave Yeah I buy properties for cash, 'course I am going to go through. No worries - my word is my bond, love."

I am not saying don't go out there and make the direct deals; do them if it works for you. But what I am saying is don't be doing them to the exclusion of all else. It is to do with risk analysis; if it only takes one Watchdog style programme to cut your business off at its knees then you need other things. Having a good relationship with your Estate Agent is one of those things then it keeps your options open.

Having a good relationship with your Estate Agent may work more slowly, but it is like an avalanche, it takes years to build the required reputation with an Estate Agent, but ten years later you will be getting the good number of the leads you want from them. It is not going to buy you the fourteen houses in six months which some of these leafleting and local advertising strategies are generating for people.

But it is still very useful and can do something else for you. Motivated vendors are inherently worried as they are going through a stressful time. Anything that you can do to make it easier for the vendor, like the Estate Agent they trust saying, "This is going to happen. This is going to go through. I have 100% faith in him. He has been doing this for twelve years," is going to make their life better. Add to that the fact that 90% of properties come up for sale through Estate Agents. There is a big pool that is currently relatively un-fished. Compare this to a comparatively small pool of motivated direct vendors and the number of Property Investors chasing them. I think that pool is becoming more and more fished out as I see more and more investors pile into that space. That sort of leafleting is very much better if you are the only person leafleting in town. Once the vendor is getting a different leaflet from a different company every week it is going to be hard to sustain.

So What Do Estate Agents Want?

In order to work with Estate Agents successfully you need to understand how they are motivated. What Estate Agents want are sales that go through. But Estate Agents with any experience realise that this is a numbers game. They want to distribute lots of details, from these they want to arrange some viewings, to get in a few offers, to get the sale through.

It is just a funnel like so many other things in this business. At the top the more sets of details distributed, the more of these will turn into viewings, the more offers you will be putting forward, the more sales they will see going through.

Sometimes the problem for Estate Agents isn't a lack of sales so much as a lack of viewings. When looking at a particular customer, the Estate Agent is quite happy that maybe he hasn't had a sale agreed yet because what he really wants is to be able to say to the vendor, "We have had four more viewings this week." This is when you can help the Estate Agent, even if you aren't going to buy, just by viewing and perhaps making a low offer. From the Estate Agent's point of view, what they are really trying to avoid is the vendor de-listing a property to list it with another agency.

If you look at why this is, it is inevitably because there hasn't been enough action. Therefore the good Estate Agent wants to be able to be in continuous contact with the vendor demonstrating that something is happening every few days, contacting the vendor with another viewing, another offer, or indicating that they have issued another thirty sets of details to people who are interested in the property.

You can help out the Estate Agents sometimes. I do genuinely get calls from my local Estate Agent saying, "Mark. Can you go round and do a viewing, and put in one of your silly low offers?" You do get this, "And oh! By the way you have no chance of getting this one Mark, but it would really help me if you could come and do a viewing tomorrow evening."

This is a case of you scratch my back – I'll scratch yours. I will go and do those viewings and often put in my low offer. Normally the Estate Agent is right, it doesn't get accepted, but then I wasn't going to get that deal anyway. On the other hand, the worst thing that can happen is that my silly low offer is accepted and I get a property for £10,000 less than it should be with a really good cash flow out of it.

Building relationships with people particularly people with the view to earning money, is not just about helping them out but helping them make money. The best way to build a relationship with an Estate Agent is to buy properties through them. Estate Agents are used to people putting on their suit and tie on a Saturday afternoon and saying, "Hi, I'm an Investor – what is your best investment property?" The Estate Agent's typical response to that, at least internally, is "No you're not. You've just been watching too much television and you think that you should be a Property Investor, a Buy-to-Letter."

Real investors don't put on their suit and tie, on a Saturday afternoon, and they don't say, "What is your best investment property?" Real Property Investors wear jeans and polo shirts, and nip in on a Thursday morning, "Is there anything interesting this week?" Have a little five minute chat, don't waste their time, just enough so they know that you are still around and interested. This helps up to a point, but what really helps is buying properties through them.

If you want Estate Agents to phone you first, you need a good track record of letting them earn their commission. Not just going in and saying, "Yeah mate, I'm an investor can you help?" Instead I say to an Estate Agent "I am looking for this kind of property."

Best Price Or Best Deal?

Remember the good, honest Estate Agents are going to pass you the good deals. The Estate Agent isn't quite obliged to get the best *price* for their vendor, Estate Agents are paid to get the best *deal* for the vendor, the right combination of Price, Speed and Security of Transaction. I know there are Estate Agents out there who put multiple offers to their clients:

1. Mrs Jones is offering £175,000. She has got a two bedroom house locally and she is going to bring me the details to put it on the market. I reckon it will take 3 months to sell, so we would look for exchange and completion in about 3 to 4 months.

OR:

2. Mr Harrison has offered not £175,000 but £165,000. He is an investor and he has got the deposit funds. He has got a good relationship with his broker, he has bought many properties through us. He has said that he can complete in 4 weeks and I know he can because he always does.

Which do they want? It is down to the vendor. The good Estate Agent will make sure that the vendor understands the options. Yes, we know that 90% of vendors will probably hold out for the higher offer - They believe that they have got time on their side and that it doesn't matter. They just want the extra £10,000 because that is all they see. The vendors who are looking for that time element, and for whom £165,000 is enough, might accept the offer. These offers come up from Estate Agents more times than many people seem to appreciate.

There are a lot of investors who say that the only way they can make money is from motivated vendors (there is a lot of truth in that) and that these motivated vendors only come up through private contacts (not always the case.)

I don't follow this logic at all. It may be that private contacts and advertising leaflets are a very efficient way to get to the motivated vendor, but it is only an efficient way to get to the ones who haven't signed up with an Estate Agent already. Generally, in this country if someone wants to sell their property the first thing they do is talk to an Estate Agent. There are many motivated vendors who use Estate Agents - they might not even have been so motivated when they first decided to sell their property. Also there are more Investors chasing the fewer motivated vendors who won't sell through Estate Agents, than there are investors who are deliberately targeting the motivated vendors selling through Estate Agents. It is a subtly different tactic.

You need to bear in mind that they will only consider the leaflets if they are motivated *at the time they decided to sell.* Don't forget that vendors often do what that vendor did in my earlier example in the "Leave The Door Open" section of Negotiation Ploys. They believed that they had got time on their side so listed the property with an Estate Agent. Over the next three to six months they backed themselves into a corner where they were suddenly more motivated; in that example they had found their dream house and they had made an offer wanted to move, but now they no longer had six months, but six weeks, and needed the sale. They could have now been getting a divorce or got a new job and need to relocate; anything that changed their circumstances. True, if the vendor is already up against it, when they decide to sell, then that is the time when they answer the adverts. But there are an awful lot more people who have done the right thing, signed up with an Estate Agent, and who now find that they are up against the wall and are in an unbreakable contract with the Estate Agent, maybe needing to give two months notice to break, time they don't have.

Don’t abandon what works for you in generating the direct contacts, but don’t focus on that way to the exclusion of any other. Realise that there are motivated vendors in both areas and catch the best deals in both areas. Opinions seem to have swung too far the other way; it used to be all Estate Agents and there were rich pickings in the direct sales market. Now there is a lot of competition in direct sales and because of that people have perhaps stopped using the Estate Agents. USE BOTH.

Building Relationships

Build relationships with everyone in the office. It is very choleric to say, "I'd like to speak to the boss!" This is the time to be more sanguine, build relationships with everyone in the office, the junior negotiator and the senior negotiator. Build the relationship with them so that they remember you when a sale is needed quickly on a property.

Sometimes things are not as they seem. There is an Estate Agent within five miles of where I live with two people in the office on the average day. There is a lady who is in her mid thirties, very power dressed, and there is a lady in her mid twenties dressed a little more casually. Who is the junior negotiator? Guess which one is the niece of the owner? The youngster. Going in and doing the "I'm only going to talk to the most important person" completely misses the fact that she is the boss's niece, and he owns a few Estate Agencies locally, and moves between them.

So look to build relationships with everyone; you don't know where the power is. Saying "I want to see the boss" and only building a good relationship with that person risks alienating everyone else. Building a relationship with everyone, will give you three allies rather that one ally and two enemies. So be careful about that – as I say it is very choleric to go in and only want to speak to the person who can get you the most deals and assume that that is the most senior person. This is not always the case.

Building up a relationship with your Estate Agent, you don't give the Estate Agent small presents, you let them give you small presents to build that rapport. Whenever I have a little bit of photocopying, either Mary or myself nip into our Estate Agent, "Mike I have a couple of papers I need to copy – our personal tax forms – I couldn't use your copier for a couple of minutes could I?" – "Yeah 'course you could Mark."

Why? – It builds up the relationship, makes him feel that you are nice to deal with. Then it is a prefect excuse at Christmas to say "Here's some bottles of wine, one for you and one for each of you in the office." This is not a thank you for putting properties my way, but a thank you for using the photocopier throughout the year. Absolutely fine, but I would never offer a cash incentive to an Estate Agent.

If they, in any way, indicated that they would accept some kind of cash incentive from me to put deals my way, they would immediately identified themselves as fundamentally dishonest. If I can not trust them to work for their client who has paid them thousands of pounds then why should I trust them to work for me when I am only paying them a couple of hundred.

Yes there are bad Estate Agents out there, we all know this, it happens and from time to time people get prosecuted. But a little gift for a little gift, the photocopying, here's a bottle of wine, absolutely fine and continually reminds the Estate Agent that you are there. I like to only buy through Estate Agents whose integrity I can trust, who I feel are genuine, honest, and open people where everyone is doing well.

I have in the past used finders, and I am quite happy to pay finders their fee, but it is very clear that they are working for me. More about finders later.

Getting Past The "I Can't Put That Offer To My Client" Block

Have you ever heard this from an Estate Agent? You have put an offer to the Estate Agent and they have said, "I can't put that offer forward, that is much too low."

Stage One

The "I can't put the offer to my client" tactic, remember it is just a negotiation ploy. However, in a very, very few cases the Estate Agent will have received an explicit instruction from a vendor along the lines of, "Do not bother putting forward to me any offers less than £160,000." In the majority of cases there will not have been any instruction, or indeed the vendor might have said, "Put forward any offers that come my way, even if it is low."

The reason they say, "I can't put the offer to my client" is because it is more convincing than <GASP>. That is ALL it is. "I can't put the offer to my client" is <GASP> spelt out long hand.

It is a negotiation ploy – disarm it. If you ever get this said to you the first thing is, to ask them to confirm it, by basically repeating it back to them as a question. "So you are saying you are not prepared to put that offer forward to your client?" At that stage, three quarters of the time you will find, no it was just a negotiation ploy, "No, no, that is not what I am saying at all – I just don't think they will accept it." Whether the Estate Agent thinks that the vendor will accept it is entirely irrelevant. I have put lots of offers in which the Estate Agents have never thought that their client will accept. - Exhibit A, the house I bought when the vendor had turned down an offer of £10,000 higher only a few weeks before. Estate Agents aren't mind readers. Stage one - disarm it.

Stage Two

Occasionally you do get the Estate Agent who says, "No, no I am not prepared to put that offer to my client." From the feedback I have had, when speaking to other Investors on this, it seems to be the case more so in London than in the rest of the country, locally to me it doesn't seem to happen. If it does happen then you ask, "Had your client instructed you not to put low offers through to them?" - If the response to this is "No, I am just not prepared to put it to my client!", say, "I would like to speak to your boss."

Stop the negotiation, talk to the boss. Say to the boss, "Are you aware that a member of your staff has just refused to put an offer through to the vendor? Clearly we have a problem here - what is going on?" Generally, at this stage the boss is likely to say, "No, no, there must be some mistake, they couldn't possibly have said that, of course we will put it forward to our client I don't understand why we are having this conversation." Invariably they put the offer out to the vendor. I have only needed to get to this stage myself.

Stage Three – The Nuclear Option

There is a stage three, it is the nuclear option. When you have got to the stage when the boss has said "No I'm not prepared to put this offer through to our client, because it is too low." Then you say, "Well look, are you telling me that you have had explicit instructions from your client not to put offers forward below a threshold". Then one of two things happen:

1. If they say, "Yes, that is the case." Then say to them, "So what kind of figure would you put forward to them?"

Easy isn't it? They are telling you that there is a Good Cop, Bad Cop situation and they are telling you in a very formal way that yes, they have received an explicit instruction. Just ask what that threshold figure is, if you are lucky, they will tell you and then it is easy. They don't always tell.

2. More often it is just the Estate Agent, "Oh I don't know what you are talking about. I can't put an offer through that low."

Then use the nuclear option, which I have known a few people use, but it is not without it's risks! You say "I know where the client lives, I know the address of the property, this afternoon I am going to be writing a letter to your client, and I am going to copy in my solicitor and you. It goes as follows, 'Dear Sir or Madam, Please be advised for your records, that I today placed an offer to purchase your property with your Estate Agent, and your Estate Agent has refused to put it to you. I thought that you should be aware of this and hence I am writing to you directly, and if you would like to discuss this offer with me please do not hesitate to call me on ….'

The upside is that the offer goes through but the downside is that it massively pisses off the Estate Agent, who tries really hard to make sure that a) the deal doesn't go through and b) tries never to sell to you again. But the kind of Estate Agents who would say, "I can't put that offer to my client," and not immediately back off are probably not the kind of Estate Agents you are going to build long term relationships with anyway.

Because I am using this as the nuclear option and making it very clear that I am not standing for this, I won't put a figure in the letter. This is for no other reason then that it allows me to start again directly with the vendor without the Estate Agent in the way. If you have the Estate Agent still in the negotiations they are never going to be helpful.

But in the long run would you want to be doing business with blatant liars? You are going to get stung no matter what you do. There are enough deals out there, and enough other Estate Agents that you can buy property very profitably through, not worry about this one. Again it is the law of averages, I don't care if this happens one in fifty times, so long as I am buying enough properties it won't matter.

Apparently somewhere in the States, at any given time, there is someone stealing from a Wal-Mart – because there are so many of stores and so much shoplifting. Statistically, there has to be someone in a Wal-Mart who is intending to walk out with a packet of biscuits, or jar of coffee or something. If that had been what Sam Walton had focused on when he started his business, then he would never have started a business that has grown in size. Instead he focused on the business not the problems. So focus on the deals we can make work and don't worry about the ones like this.

Caution with the Nuclear Option

The nuclear option – if you have got to the stage of telling their client that they haven't put offers through then you are going to have problems.

Offers In Writing

When dealing through Estate Agents, should you put offers in writing or not? I think that when you are dealing with private vendors, dropping them a little letter to confirm the offer, so that they can see it, has great impact.

But with Estate Agents – I'm not so sure. The Estate Agents that I have ended up working with long term know where I am and I know they are putting it through to their clients, because I am seeing deals coming through my way. I don't particularly feel the need to write as I know that, over the next three or four days, negotiations will be going back and forth with offers and counter offers anyway. Also I am only dealing with Estate Agents who, I know, once an offer has been verbally accepted, will be writing a letter to me and posting it the following day (required under the Estate Agency Act) "For your records here is the offer agreed..."

If you don't get this letter specified by the Estate Agency Act the following morning, then you should start being slightly worried. If it hasn't come in forty-eight hours time you should be very, very worried. I have always had a written confirmation, from the Estate Agent, of any verbal agreement. Then we know that every party has got written confirmation of the agreement; this is powerful because you know that the vendor has also received a letter stating, "This is to confirm that you have agreed to sell ...." – it may not be any more legally binding then a piece of paper which has "The Numberjacks are

On Their Way" [7]written on it, but emotionally and psychologically it is powerful. You should always make sure that the Estate Agents are sending through the confirmations. As this paperwork is being done anyway I tend not to put the offers in writing when I am dealing through Estate Agents.

7 If you are UK-based, and have small children, then you'll understand.

Finders Versus Estate Agents

I have been asked if I would offer an Estate Agent a fee for passing details of properties to me first, as there are presumably other investors also approaching the same Estate Agents.

If Estate Agents are accepting money from both the vendor and the purchaser they are breaching the Estate Agency Act and are committing a criminal offence; as they are not acting in the best interests of their client. I don't want to do business with the kind of people who would accept bribes. A key difference between a finder's fee and a bribe is that you can't get sent to prison for accepting a finders fee. The Estate Agency Act makes it very clear that once the Estate Agent has signed a contract and entered into a sale agreement with the vendor, they must then act in the vendor's best interests. If the Estate Agent is paid to work for me, then I want him working for me and not the other party. If I find out later that the Estate Agent had been accepting cash in brown envelopes then I would be banging on his office door with my lawyers.

The kind of Estate Agents who are accepting these 'Finder's Fees' are setting themselves up for big problems and at the very least will find that people like me won't buy through them. I refuse to work with people who are dishonest.

Are they a Finder or an Estate Agent? If they are Sourcing Agents (or Finders) then that is what they do. That is their job. They work for the buyers, they have a legal obligation to work for their buyer. If you have two buyers they sell their services to the highest bidder.

If, they are Estate Agents – Estate Agents in the UK – they work for vendors. That is what the Estate Agency Act says; if you are being paid money to sell a property then there is a legal obligation to do the best for your client, the vendor. Estate Agents are not allowed to accept money from another party.

Sourcing Agents are very different people. Often confusion comes because sometimes they operate out of Estate Agent offices. But no agent is allowed to represent both parties in one transaction.

Dealing With Property Developers

Property Developers In General.

This is like dealing with Estate Agents in that it has become so tarnished over the last couple of years that many investors don't want to do it because of the problems we have seen. Again, I think that we are going to see a growth of useful deals coming through as the market improves. Obviously we are no longer in a booming market and developers have stopped assuming that they can sell everything with a 15% gifted deposit.

So, don't rule dealing with developers completely out of your armoury. It is, maybe, not one to go for quite yet but, over the next year or two, it might be worth starting to approach them again. Again it is about using each pool. There are pools of directly contacted motivated vendors, people who are looking to sell through Estate Agents, and new–build properties. Restricting yourself to just one of these pools is always going to be dangerous. But understanding, and mixing all three, is more likely to land you consistently good catches.

Sales Targets

The motivation for developers is about sale targets. In the UK the majority of UK properties are built by one of the big nationally listed housing development companies: Taywood, Alfred McAlpines, etc. These companies have got quarterly and annual targets which they have to report to the Stock Exchange. The companies want to be able to report good sales and sales growth each quarter. So their staff also have matching targets.

It is a good idea when you are looking to buy from a particular developer to find out which month their reporting targets fall in. Then go in about four weeks before hand and say, "Look I can do this, and complete by the end of June." If this means that the deal can complete (or some companies measure it, exchange contracts) by the end of June, as an investor this is part of you armoury, then actually it can be included in that reporting month's figures. Even better, the salesman will meet their personal bonus target. The regional commercial director will meet their target, etc. and the company is able to report it to the Stock Market.

So understand that if this sale can fall into the earlier period rather than the next one, this can sometimes be useful in getting great deals.

Respect "Mah Authority"

Again the authority issue comes into it. Remember that front-line staff in builders' sales offices or marketing suites have some negotiation room, but not much. Typically these days on a £200,000 property, they will probably have £10,000, lets say 5% that they can agree there and then.

Some developers may give their front-line staff maybe 10% or even 15%. These discounts are achievable if you can commit to exchanging in 28 days and write out a deposit cheque for £1,000 there and then, which you loose if you haven't exchanged in that 28 days.

To get bigger discounts than this, then of course you need to go up the chain. Imagine the scenario:

You say, "I don't want to talk to you I want to talk to your commercial director."

The commercial director is quite likely to say, "So you want 15% discount – so how many are you buying?"

"One."

"So why are you wasting my time?"

If you want to be getting bigger discounts from developers then you need to be buying significant numbers of properties. This is partly why these buying syndicates, or buying off plan companies were started and why some of them are actually quite useful.

I had a call about eighteen months ago, out of the blue, from someone in East Anglia, asking about a local company which is a portfolio building company based in Crawley. He wondered, as I came from Crawley, had I heard anything about this company, which yes I had - I had bought a couple of places through them – "Well what do you think of them?"

"They are terribly well meaning, but they tend to get carried away. They don't always research the rents terribly well. At the end of the day they will give you the discounts that they have said but don't believe the things they say in terms of rental income."

"Don't worry about that, you have just told me all I need to know"

"Oh, How?"

"Well I live in Ipswich and there is a development of city centre flats here, I want to buy one. I have been into the Sales Office to get the best deal I can push out of the sales lady there. But I was doing a bit of surfing on the web and I saw that they could get me the same flat for (even after their fees) a few grand less. I have no interest in rental potential as I just want to live there; I just wanted to check that they weren't crooks that were going to take my initial fees and run away. They can genuinely get me a better deal than I can get myself."

Well good luck to him! These kinds of property building portfolio companies can be great. I know that they have got a bit of a bad reputation but that is often for – shall we say – being over optimistic about the rent predictions. The reason they can achieve far higher discounts is because they are putting together a consortium of investors, who, between them, are looking to buy a significant proportion of the development.

This happens all the time in commercial property. The average new build London block of flats (a single block in which there are thirty or more units) is, on average, bought and sold about five times between the planning stage to the first people moving in. Generally, something like the following will happen - the big pension funds and builders buy it at the planning stage to sell it on at the next stage in development. Or pension funds who have bought the site initially will sell it on at double the price to a Far East consortium once it has been granted planning permission. They in turn, sell it on to someone else, who packages it down, ten units here, ten units there, thirty units to be sold off in the marketing suite, and five units sold individually, etc.

This consortia buying and selling is not unusual; it is actually very common at the commercial level. But, as an individual investor, it is harder because you need to be buying so many units to get the discounts that go with them.

Opportunities - When Buying 1 Or 2 New-Build Properties

The question for most of us is how do we get a good deal from the builder when we are only buying one or perhaps just two properties. There are some opportunities. At the start of the build, when the "Land Acquired for" boards first go up, or the day the marketing suite opens is often a very good day to go in there and say, "What are they going to sell for? We are thinking of buying some." What these companies love is to be able to say, "30% already sold," when they put up the 'For Sale' banners.

If they can open the marketing suite and – bam – 30% already sold even before our show flat opens that automatically generates a lot of interest from the 'I've got to get the foot on the ladder' crowd, who then pile in. That is why they are interested in getting the percentage of deals agreed and not so worried about the extra 5% or 10% on those individual properties; because they know that in the long run they can advertise those sales, and get much better prices on the remaining 70%.

Also, at the end of the build, they want to sell that last unsold flat quickly because as long as it has not sold, they are having to keep the marketing suite running, paying one or two people to be there. They are heating it and lighting it when they want to be out of there and down the road. Or even worse they ARE out of there and down the road and the last one is hard to sell because they have closed the marketing suite. So at the end of the build developers are sometimes willing to accept a low offer.

I got a fantastic tip from a friend of mine who buys new-build properties in the Cambridgeshire area, not off plan but just as cash flow properties. Whenever she encounters a rude sales person in a marketing suite she knows that she is laughing all the way to the bank. She has discovered that when the sales person is rude or just not very good at their job a few months tends to go by and very little will have been sold. The Marketing Department then send someone in basically as a troubleshooter to try and get the properties sold. By this time the building company is so desperate to get the sales in quickly that an extra five or ten grand less on each property is acceptable.

So there are opportunities to be had when buying from developers; at the start of the build, at the end of the build and when you encounter a rude or unprofessional sales person.

Getting Someone Else To Do It

Using a Third Party?.

The final tip is basically getting someone else to do it. It is interesting that we are now seeing teams of people who are getting together to do this. The reason for this, is partly, the power thing. It is very easy to go into a negotiation and say "I have got some pre-set boundaries which have been set by ..." – and whether you say the boss or the business partner, directors or investors, is very much up to you, and really doesn't matter. With the rest of the team setting certain boundaries, it actually makes your life much easier as a negotiator because, even if you let your emotions do get in the way, you know that the rest of the team will not let you go any further anyway. They are just going to say, "No!"

Sometimes I send my brother round to make offers. He can't be bullied into doing anything else or make any changes. If I have accidentally let slip that I am the decision maker then I will quite often send him (as I will be mysteriously away on business) saying, "Mark asked me to pop round with this." It doesn't need to be someone you pay to do it. It has got to be someone who, deliberately has got lower authority as that actually gives them power because of the lack of authority. Utterly bizarre and counter intuitive, but never the less useful.

This is exactly how people use Estate Agents, I would like you to take offers on my behalf but then leave the decision up to me. The only time really that you should get in a third party and say, "You take over responsibility for that," tends to be when that other party clearly knows more about it then you do, but he is a professional and he will charge you quite high fees to do it.

Again, this generally only really happens in commercial property deals.

I spent three years working for one of the UK's largest construction companies and the division I was responsible for was building petrol stations. Building petrol stations probably doesn't sound terribly exciting until you work out that this company alone has construction costs of around $700 million a year - building petrol stations - and that doesn't include the land costs. The deal we had arranged with them was that we would get a relatively small fee plus 10% of the savings. The saving in the first year was $200 million, They gave us back $20 million as a fee, so they made to total $180 million saving. When the numbers are that big, you can afford to pay someone a $20 million fee and still walk away $180 million better off.

Property Negotiation

In Property Negotiations, where you are generally buying only one property, the numbers are seldom big enough to make paying someone else to do it worth while; particularly given that actually you don't want a sale unless it is going to make you a profit and also leave your reputation intact. The danger of getting someone else to negotiate for you is that they will feel that if they are doing their job properly they need to close every deal for you. This is absolutely not doing their job properly. Doing the job properly is closing the one in ten; the negotiation is part of the filtering process.

Don't hand over the keys to your business to someone else just because you perceive that is something that they can offer commercially for you.

Just because someone else might do a negotiation slightly better doesn't mean it will always be cost-effective to use them.

However, when negotiating larger or more complex deals, a good negotiator can be worth their fee many times over.

Appendices

Psychometric Test.

The following pages may be photocopied as required, for the purposes of assessing your psychological personality type, and that of your family members and colleagues. If you have trouble understanding any of the words please refer to the word definitions supplied.

You can download additional copies of the test from www.yournegotiationexpert.com/bonus.

Part 1 -Your Strengths

Risk taker	Spirited	Tranquil	Chart maker
Mover	Vivacious	Responsive	Courteous
Leader	Impulsive	Contented	Considerate
Intrepid	Convivial	Adaptable	Idealistic
Productive	Amusing	Tactful	Perfectionist
Competitive	Promoter	Reserved	Well Conducted
Determined	Inspiring	Dry wit	Methodical
Competent	Eager	Accepting	Loyal
Self-sufficient	Zestful	Peacemaker	Cultured
Unreserved	Cheerful	Predictable	Introspective
Enterprising	Raconteur	Restrained	Staunch
Rational	Exuberant	Accommodating	Compassionate
Forceful	Touchy-feely	Easy going	Structured
Unhesitating	Engaging	Pleasant	Mindful of others
Kingpin	Bubbly	Stable	Strategist
Self-confident	Favourite	Listener	Self-sacrificing
Independent	Sociable	Tolerant	Diligent
Decisive	Eloquent	Quiet	Meticulous
Confident	Centre of attention	Patient	Musical
Commanding	Upbeat	Acquiescent	Analytical

Part 2 -Your Weaknesses

Argumentative	Forgetful	Shrinking	Suspicious
Exploitive	Sloppy	Mutters	Negative
Sly	Talkative	Tentative	Easily offended
Overbearing	Booming	Faint-hearted	Cut off
Intolerant	Repetitious	Poker face	Reclusive
Workaholic	Erratic	Apprehensive	Over critical
Undiplomatic	Restless	Indolent	Pessimistic
Quick-tempered	Giddy	Yielding	Surly
Hasty	Unmethodical	Doubting Outcome	Isolated
Pig headed	Short attention span	Prosaic	Insecure
Reckless	Temper tantrums	Unenthusiastic	Unpopular
Imperious	Interrupts	Purposeless	Self conscious
Resistant	Showy	Not Interested	Introvert
Arrogant	Chaotic	Anxious	Depressed
Undemonstrative	Craves approval	Dilly dallying	Bitter
Tactless	Indulgent	Apathetic	Nit picking
Unfeeling	Exhibitionist	Indecisive	Distrustful
Overconfident	Fickle	Procrastinating	Vindictive
Belligerent	Superficial	Indifferent	Holds Grudges
Self-important	Disorderly	Non committal	Judgemental

Word Definitions

These definitions are included to help you understand the words used in the psychometric test.

Accepting	Readily satisfied with the circumstances or situation.
Accommodating	Quick to fall in with another's way.
Acquiescent	Accepting of others' points of view, rarely asserting their own.
Adaptable	Will fit into any situation easily and comfortably.
Amusing	Good sense of humour, good at telling funny stories.
Analytical	Will examine things, so they can understand the logic involved.
Anxious	Always worrying and unsure about things.
Apathetic	Uninterested in other people's lives or joining organisations.
Apprehensive	Feels deep anxiety and fear.
Argumentative	Will start arguments, is unable to see others' points of view as valid.
Arrogant	Values self highly always seeing themselves as right and best at everything.

Belligerent	Insistent on their way, and their way only.
Bitter	Holds on to ill feeling from real or imagined slights.
Booming	Can be heard over everyone else at a loud party.
Bubbly	Extremely lively and energetic personality.
Centre of attention	Is adored and likes to be at the hub of the action.
Chaotic	Unable to order their time, or their life.
Chart maker	Uses lists and spreadsheets to help organise their life and work.
Cheerful	Naturally smiling and helping others to be happy.
Commanding	A forceful person, others hesitate to argue with.
Compassionate	Cares, sensitive to others.
Competent	Able to act efficiently and successfully in most circumstances.
Competitive	Makes every event a contest, and always aims to triumph.
Confident	Assured of own capability and in no doubt of winning.

Considerate	Thoughtful of others, remembers anniversaries and swiftly offers a kindness.
Contented	Seldom envious of others, happy with what he has.
Convivial	Good at a party, treats new people as old friends.
Courteous	Treats others with respect and consideration.
Craves approval	Seeks and thrives on the praise of others.
Cultured	Sophisticated and refined pastimes, visiting galleries and attending classical concerts etc.
Cut Off	Withdraws into themselves, needs time alone.
Decisive	Swift judge of situations, chooses quickly
Depressed	Consistently feels down in the dumps.
Determined	Stubborn, won't stop until a goal is achieved.
Diligent	Completes one task before starting next.
Dilly dallying	Slow to act, lazy, can't be bothered.
Disorderly	Little discipline to enable them to order any part of their lives.
Distrustful	Wary of others, and their ideas, or actions.
Doubting outcome	Uncertain of things turning out successfully.

Dry Wit	Comes up with ironic one liners.
Eager	Keen, vigorous.
Easily offended	Too sensitive to others' opinions, which they often misconstrue.
Easy going	Pleasant and friendly to be around.
Eloquent	Able to charm others into accepting their proposals.
Engaging	A person who is fun to be around.
Enterprising	Willing to take on new ventures, and determined to succeed.
Erratic	Contradictory, inconsistent actions or emotions.
Exhibitionist	Frequently showing off, needs an audience.
Exploitive	Manages others to meet their agenda.
Exuberant	Overflowing with life, lively, animated.
Faint-hearted	Timid, avoids difficult situations.
Favourite	Popular person, the A-list person on everyone's guest list.
Fickle	Unpredictable, tendency to break promises.
Forceful	Determined to have their way.

Forgetful	Doesn't remember things, especially doesn't bother to memorise boring things.
Giddy	Volatile, scatterbrained, tends to be flighty.
Hasty	Impatient, irritated by delays, or waiting for others.
Holds grudges	Has difficulty forgiving injustices done them.
Idealistic	Sees things as perfect, and strives to achieve that standard themselves.
Imperious	Bossy, domineering and overbearing.
Impulsive	Not restricted by rules, is spontaneous.
Indecisive	Has trouble making choices (not just slow to do so).
Independent	Able to rely on their own abilities and considered opinions.
Indifferent	Couldn't care less if things are one way or another.
Indolent	Sluggish, weighs up the amount of energy required to achieve anything.
Indulgent	Courts popularity by allowing others to do anything they please.
Insecure	Lacks self-confidence, apprehensive.

Inspiring	Motivating others to participate with enjoyment.
Interrupts	Talks, rather than listens, will speak without realising someone else was already doing so.
Intolerant	Lacking acceptance of others' points of view or actions.
Intrepid	Unafraid of taking risks, daring.
Introspective	Deep, intense person, dislikes small talk.
Introvert	Directs their interests and ideas inwards, emotionally self contained.
Isolated	Insecure in others' company, fearful of others' opinion of them.
Judgemental	Looks closely into everything, often finding fault.
Kingpin	Acts as chief and expects to be obeyed.
Leader	Naturally acts as the one in charge, can't see success with anyone else being in charge.
Listener	Always willing to hear what other people say.
Loyal	Faithful to another person, principles, or employer.
Methodical	A person who is disciplined, neat and tidy.

Meticulous	Painstakingly thorough, remembering events in detail.
Mindful of others	Caring about others' needs and feelings.
Mover	Driven to be productive, natural leader.
Musical	Appreciates music as an art, rather than merely the fun of taking part.
Mutters	Mumbles to themselves when cornered, won't speak out clearly.
Negative	Seldom has a positive attitude, often seeing only the dark side of a situation.
Nit picking	Finicky, tends to concentrate intensely on trivial details.
Non-committal	Hesitant to get moving, or get involved.
Not interested	Indifferent, unconcerned, laid back approach to life.
Over critical	Hard to please, sets their standards impossibly high.
Overbearing	Takes charge of any situation, will boss people about.
Overconfident	Full of guts, to the point of madness.
Patient	Not worried by hold-ups and stays unruffled.

Peacemaker	Persistently tries to act as mediator to avoid conflict.
Perfectionist	Gives themselves (and others) high standards, always wants everything to be just so.
Pessimistic	Might hope for the best, but expects the worst scenario.
Pig-headed	Determined to have their way, hard to convince otherwise, obstinate.
Pleasant	Doesn't like to act or cause offence.
Poker face	Dead-pan, expressing no emotion.
Predictable	Always does what you expect them to do.
Procrastinating	Slow to start something, will put things off.
Productive	Works long and late, consistently achieving, rarely rests.
Promoter	Attracts others, encouraging them to join in.
Prosaic	Shows little emotion, very stable temperament.
Purposeless	No desire to set goals, aimless.
Quick-tempered	Demanding, short fuse, easily angered when others are not fast enough.
Quiet	Shy, doesn't begin conversations.

Raconteur	Can easily tell stories and entertain others, uncomfortable with silence.
Rational	Uses logic and fact, rather than charm, to convince others.
Reckless	Too impatient to think before acting, rash.
Reclusive	Avoids other people, loner, solitary.
Repetitious	Says the same thing over and over without realising.
Reserved	Refrains from expressing enthusiasm or own emotions.
Resistant	Hesitates to accept any other way but their own.
Responsive	Seldom initiates a conversation but will respond to one.
Restless	Constantly looking for new stimulations, easily bored with the same things.
Restrained	Rarely displays their own emotions.
Risk taker	Adventurous, willing to take chances.
Self-confident	Knows that, when in charge, things will work out correctly.
Self-conscious	Shyly avoids catching anyone's attention.

Self-important	Tends to be pompous, expects others to defer to them.
Self-sacrificing	Willingly helps others without thought to own position.
Self-sufficient	Self-reliant, rarely needing outside assistance.
Short attention span	Lacks the powers of concentration to stick to one thing at a time, flighty.
Showy	Brash and over loud.
Shrinking	Doesn't want to get involved, particularly with complicated tasks.
Sloppy	Always in a mess, mislays things.
Sly	Shrewd, will astutely resolve a situation to get their desired result.
Sociable	Treats being with others as time for enjoyment instead of business.
Spirited	Full of excitement, and the joys of life.
Stable	Balanced personality, not given to a roller-coaster of emotions.
Staunch	Steadfast and reliable, can be overly devoted without reason.
Strategist	Prefers to be involved in working out plans for attainment of a goal, rather than carrying out the plan.

Structured	Makes daily plans, and dislikes their plans to be disrupted.
Superficial	Skims the surface of life, doesn't delve into the deeper meanings of life.
Surly	Seldom excited, easily falls into black moods.
Suspicious	Questions the intentions of others.
Tactful	Sensitive and diplomatic when dealing with others.
Tactless	Causes offence by the inconsiderate way they express themselves.
Talkative	Won't shut up, rarely stops to listen.
Temper tantrums	Easily angered, but quickly over and forgotten.
Tentative	Reluctant to take the plunge.
Tolerant	Accepts what others do and say, doesn't see a need to change them.
Touchy-feely	Demonstrative, tactile and caressing.
Tranquil	Seems peaceful and serene, avoids strife.
Undemonstrative	Has difficulty conveying affection.
Undiplomatic	Outspoken, will say whatever they think.
Unenthusiastic	Doesn't get excited, expects failure.

Unfeeling	Has little sympathy for others' problems.
Unhesitating	Sure, prompt and unwavering.
Unmethodical	Haphazard, no consistent method of achieving things.
Unpopular	Drives others away by being too demanding and intense.
Unreserved	Outspoken and candid.
Upbeat	Optimistic, believing and convincing others that things will go well.
Vindictive	Subtly spiteful, takes their revenge by punishing others.
Vivacious	Full of life, fun and good humour.
Well conducted	Likes to behave within, what they perceive as, the proper bounds.
Workaholic	Always active, pursues activity over results, feels guilty if resting.
Yielding	Avoids tension by compromising, giving up ground even when right.
Zestful	Invigorating and makes others feel good.

Items For Sale - Flinch & <Gasp> Practice.

Our corporate motto is "Have Fun, Make Money" - so we spent some time coming up with some items for you to sell to your partner.

1. Used plastic supermarket bag featuring a logo, a broken handle and a hole in the side (several designs available).
2. Energy saving light bulb.
3. Bottle of your grandmother's perfume, still in the original packaging, circa 1970.
4. Fake-gold-plated fountain pen, with engraved initials, and inscription 'For a Job Well Done'.
5. Second-hand tombstone, ideal for person named John Doe, 1945-2004.
6. One hundred shares in Enron.
7. A sheaf of second-hand advertisements for new models of mobile phone – ideal for shredding and use as bedding for a small rodent.
8. Second-hand book "Lives of the great Accountants, volume 4".
9. Anything sent to you by the Her Majesty's Customs and Revenue (formerly the Inland Revenue and Customs and Excise.)
10. A trial CD from any Internet Service Provider.

Recommended Reading

Read our reviews, and get an updated list at

- www.yournegotiationexpert.com/books

Freakonomics, Steven D. Levitt and Stephen J. Dubner

- A layman's guide to economics, including the research about US realtors selling their own houses.

Getting to Yes, Roger Fisher et al

- The very first book on negotiation I ever read.

Essential Negotiation, Gavin Kennedy

- The Economist 's A-Z guide of negotiation terms – not an easy read, but well recommended.

The E-Myth Revisited, Michael E. Gerber

- A must-read for anyone thinking of setting up a business, property or otherwise.

Why business people speak like idiots, Brian Fugere et al

- The inspiration for the “style” of this book.

Training Courses

We run a one-day workshop called “Property Negotiation”. You can find details of the next dates and venues at our website.

www.yournegotiationexpert.com

However, as an existing customer of this book, you are entitled to a special discount on the course, so if you want to attend, drop us an email to the special address below, tell us when you bought the book, and we'll negotiate a better price with you.

You can mail us on the special address “IboughtTheBook@yournegotiationexpert.com . At that point, we'll see how good a deal you can negotiate on the course price!

Obviously, the better a deal you can negotiate, the less you need the course, so it's only fair that you pay less for it !

You can also sign up for our free newsletter about UK Property Investment at www.yourpropertyexpert.com

Good luck!

www.ingramcontent.com/pod-product-compliance
Ingram Content Group UK Ltd.
Pitfield, Milton Keynes, MK11 3LW, UK
UKHW021043200726
13857UKWH00003B/787

9 781847 538451